Tom - Merry Christmas
Hope you will enJoy -

John Spencer
1996

WITHDRAWN

No Place Like Lowe's

~

50 Years of Retailing for the American Home

For everyone
who enjoys a good yarn
and a good day's work
in good company.

1996 Sales Meeting, Opryland Hotel, Nashville, Tennessee

Copyright © 1996 Lowe's Companies, Inc.
Cliff Oxford, Publisher
Box 1111
Highway 268 East (Elkin Highway)
North Wilkesboro, NC 28656

Printed in the United States of America by Quebecor Printing, Kingsport, TN

Printing Coordinator: Matt Phelan of Phelan Communications Inc., Atlanta, GA

Pre-press Production:
Charles and Robert Sappington
Computer Tree/Digital Publishing,
Winston-Salem, NC

McIntyre, Deni, 1955-
No Place Like Lowe's

1. Lowe's-History

Library of Congress Catalog
Card Number: 96-69933

ISBN 0-9653801-0-6

No Place Like Lowe's

50 Years of Retailing for the American Home

Text by Deni McIntyre
Photography and photo research by Will McIntyre
Design and illustration by Henry Church

The Forties

Leonard Herring flicked an invisible dust speck from the hood of his new postwar Chevy and leaned casually against the fender. The guys would be out in a minute, then they'd hit the road. On Friday afternoons there was steady traffic through the Chi Psi house on Cameron Avenue, as frat brothers ditched textbooks and jackets in favor of footballs and sweatshirts. Some, like Leonard and his buddies, were heading out from Chapel Hill to meet friends at another campus. Others were planning nothing more ambitious than a movie at the Carolina Theater on Franklin Street, or a cold beer at Danziger's.

Even parked behind the frat house, Leonard's Chevy got plenty of attention from passers-by. Manufacturing lines had not yet caught up with the heavy postwar demand for new automobiles, and the 1946 Chevy was something that most people had seen only on display floors or in magazines. Some persuasive arguments had been aired so that this nineteen-year-old commerce major could own this car. Leonard heard, and learned, and kept his own counsel. Someday he would be the one who knew how to get things done.

Gordon Cadwgan jammed his hands deeper into his trouser pockets and lengthened his stride down Westminster Street in Providence, trying to walk off his frustration. Sometimes it seemed that the Navy had taken more than its share of his life. While he was trailing MacArthur around the Philippines on an amphibious landing ship known to its crew as the "Snafu Maru," his family had grown from two children to three. He missed baby Gordon's birth (although only by two days); then this spring, when May brought the children to pick him up in Boston after his dis-

The original Lowe's North Wilkesboro Hardware on C Street, with adjacent buildings acquired for expansion.

charge, little Carol stood in the back seat on the way home and asked "Mommy, who is this man?" Well, they were a family again now. But back at the brokerage firm of G.H. Walker, someone else was handling all the business he'd built up before the war. It was tough making cold calls, talking to new companies, fighting for a toehold all over again. As a deck officer on the Snafu Maru, he had been in charge of damage control. He hadn't known then how much damage control he would be doing in civilian life!

Bobby Strickland tucked his books under his arm, grabbed his clarinet case, and caught the screen door just before it slammed behind him. It wouldn't take him ten minutes to walk the four blocks to Asheboro High, especially with last night's boogie-woogie still percolating in his head. The dance band was sounding pretty tight, he thought, considering they hadn't played together all summer. Pretty soon they'd start looking for some Friday night gigs— which would be okay with his mother, probably, as long as he could get enough sleep before his Saturday job clerking at the appliance store downtown.

Max Freeman and his wife, Ann, had spent one last night at the cottage on the shores of Lake Hickory. They spent it in the little two-man trailer that was already hooked behind their old Buick. The cottage was sold; Max and Ann were ready to leave.

Their decision hadn't been an easy one, but managing the little community's water system had become a bigger headache than it was worth. Clay Swain, who ran the airport at Salisbury where Max was flying part-time, had said "Max, you've got to decide: are you going to stay in aviation, or are you going to sell mops?" That did it: Max was one flyboy who hadn't gotten it all out of his system during the war. If he couldn't fly B-29's or Air Corps tankers, he would fly twin Cessnas and Beechcrafts for anybody from Havana to Boston who needed a good pilot.

There had been a tremendous storm during the night. Flood water had rushed down a hillside and filled the community well with sand. Everybody was out of water, but now— finally— it was someone else's problem. Max and Ann climbed into the Buick and waved good-bye.

Mary Marsh was five years old and on her way to school. She was registered in the first grade at Union

Top: Chapel Hill frat man Leonard Herring and his 1946 Chevy before the Carolina-Maryland football game.
Bottom: When Gordon Cadwgan came home from the Navy, he had to make up for lost time— both personal and professional.

Elementary in North Wilkesboro, about a half mile from her home in the Cricket Community. She wasn't a bit scared; she wanted to go. Then her parents got a call from the authorities. There were too many first graders for the old wooden schoolhouse that year; could Mary wait and start again next year?

Mary was disappointed. Her mother, who was caring for a two-year-old son at home anyway, didn't let her feelings show. Mary stayed home and looked after her little brother, rode her tricycle up and down the gravel driveway, and played in the creek in the woods behind their house. The old schoolhouse would be replaced by a new brick building the year Mary entered second grade.

Petro Kulynych walked up C Street in North Wilkesboro, stopped opposite the post office, and for the first time crossed the threshold of Lowe's North Wilkesboro Hardware. It was a typical hardware store for a rural North Carolina community, stocked with rolls of barbed wire, kegs of nails, galvanized roofing, and some plumbing supplies. The horse collars and harnesses hanging on the walls were meant to be functional, not decorative. The lone salesman, a nice looking fellow, pointed Pete to a rear corner of the store, where plywood panels defined a makeshift office. Pete took a deep breath and went in.

Two men were sitting at a big double desk, counting money and stuffing it in bags. One wore thick eyeglasses with dark frames that gave him an intense, somewhat owlish look. The other was a big man with a head of curly black hair. They would both be about his age, Pete thought— maybe a few years older.

It was the big man, Jim Lowe, who spoke. "What the hell do you want?"

Pete held out a card with the store's address handwritten on it, along with a name— Carl Buchan. "I got this from Mr. Kirkpatrick at King's Business College in Charlotte. He said you were looking for a bookkeeper." Carl Buchan, the man in glasses, leaned back in his chair and nodded.

"You know how to keep books?" Jim Lowe asked.

Top: In the fall of 1946, Mary Marsh (here with brother Ike) was ready for school, but the overcrowded North Wilkesboro school system wasn't ready for her.
Middle: Roena and Pete Kulynych during his days as a cadet midshipman in the Merchant Marine Academy, c. 1943. He later enlisted in the Navy and was a full lieutenant by the time of his discharge in 1945.
Bottom: Bob Strickland played clarinet in his school band, saxophone in a dance band, and clerked in an appliance store on weekends.

Photo by Will McIntyre

"Yes, sir!" It wasn't exactly true; Pete had never kept a set of books in his life. But he had been studying accounting down in Charlotte, and he desperately needed this job. Besides, he thought, look at these guys— sharing a desk, stuffing cash in bags, and using an old Monroe hand calculator that must have weighed fifty pounds. Sales tickets with running accounts were stuck on the wall behind the desk. Pete thought, I could make myself useful here.

"All right, you can have the job," Jim Lowe said. "It pays $25.40 a week, plus whatever you get on the G.I. bill."

Pete Kulynych became Lowe's first bookkeeper on November 15, 1946.

Most early settlers of the Carolina back country came south on the Great Philadelphia Wagon Road. In the fertile valley of the Yadkin River they raised cattle, pigs, and a variety of row crops. The Catawba and Cherokee nations had fished, hunted, and planted corn there for generations, but their towns began to disappear as the European settlements multiplied.

Wilkes County, North Carolina was created in 1778 from part of Surry County on the southeast slopes of the Blue Ridge Mountains. It was named to honor a member of England's Parliament who had sided with the American colonies during the revolution. A county courthouse was built in a central location just south of the Yadkin River, and gradually the town of Wilkesboro grew up around it.

Wilkes County was isolated from the more populous and progressive Piedmont region by poor roads and the fact that the Yadkin didn't lend itself to profitable navigation. But as the furniture industry became more important to the Piedmont, demand grew for lumber and bark from Wilkes County, which led to talk of a railroad.

The Richmond and Danville Rail Road Company was contracted to build a railroad to Wilkesboro from the town of Rural Hall fifty miles east. To arrive in Wilkesboro proper, it would have to bridge the Yadkin; but the company's engineers decided to avoid the expense of a bridge by ending the line across the river from Wilkesboro, at a place that had been known first as

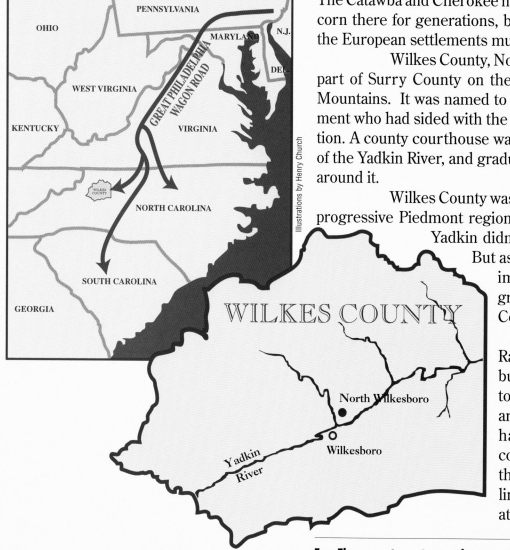

Illustrations by Henry Church

Top: The current county courthouse on Main Street in Wilkesboro was built by the WPA in the 1930's.
Bottom: Lowe's birthplace was a small town in a rural county in northwestern North Carolina.

the Mulberry Fields, then as Fairmount, then Gordon. The Winston Land and Improvement Company, which held options on land around the site designated for the depot, decreed that the place should be renamed North Wilkesboro.

North Wilkesboro became the county's industrial center; Wilkesboro remained its political hub. North Wilkesboro generally voted Democratic; Wilkesboro was Republican. Resentment and rivalry were inevitable as North Wilkesboro's growth outpaced the county seat's. Some attempts were made to consolidate the two, but in 1891 the town of North Wilkesboro was incorporated.

By 1920, the town's industries included C.C. Smoot & Sons Tannery, the Wilkes Hosiery Mill, and the Home Chair Company. That year marked the start of Prohibition, which encouraged development of an even better-known Wilkes County industry: the manufacture and sale of bootleg whiskey.

In 1921, Warren G. Harding became the 29th President of the United States; the Union of Soviet Socialist Republics was established; inflatable tires were invented for the automobile; and L. S. Lowe opened Lowe's North Wilkesboro Hardware. Lucius Lowe and his wife had three daughters and a son. The family business thrived in a modest way; when Lucius died in 1940, he left it to his daughter Ruth. She immediately sold out to her brother, Jim, for $4200. Her future lay elsewhere, she thought—with a certain young man from the Sandhills. His name was Carl Buchan.

"Don't sit under the apple tree with anyone else but me . . . "
Top: Across the nation, the end of the war was the signal to warm up church organs, as G.I.'s traded the quick march for the Wedding March.
Right: Army paratrooper Don Gladieux married his hometown hula girl in 1946. Later he would become a Lowe's contractor customer in Hendersonville, North Carolina.

Gladieux Family Collection

Gladieux Family Collection

Although completely unknown in clannish Wilkes County, the Buchan name meant a lot around Southern Pines. The Buchans were pioneer settlers of the Sandhills area. Carl's grandfather, John, owned a big cotton plantation in southern Moore County; John's son, H. C. Buchan, seemed destined to follow in his father's footsteps. He earned a degree from State College (now N.C. State University) and did some graduate work in agriculture at Auburn.

He married Marie Godfrey of Jonesboro, and together they had five sons. But instead of farming, H.C. started his own trucking company. Buchan Motor Lines hauled goods for the A&P grocery chain and prospered for a while, but went bust during the Depression. Marie died in 1934, and the four younger boys went to live with an aunt in Pinebluff. The oldest boy, Carl, was eighteen by then, a State College student with journalistic ambitions. He left college to take a job as a newspaper reporter in Asheboro, but soon found himself drawn to the advertising department. There was something about selling that appealed to young Carl Buchan.

When he met Ruth Lowe, he was working for a finance company out of Charlotte. By 1941, however, the newlyweds had moved to Kinston, where Carl was selling the freight services of the Atlantic and East Coast Rail Road. His brother John, who lived with the couple in Kinston for a while, says that Carl liked the job and was good at it. "But then, he was good at everything he tried," John recalls.

Was anyone in America unaffected by the events of December 7, 1941? After Pearl Harbor, everyone's plans changed. All five Buchan boys went into service; so did Ruth Buchan's brother, Jim Lowe. Carl Buchan graduated from Officer Candidate School at Camp Lee, Virginia and was sent to an army quartermaster corps in Texas. Ruth moved back to North Wilkesboro to help her mother run the hardware store while Jim served as an instructor in the air corps.

In 1942, the lyrics to Duke Ellington's "Don't Get Around Much Anymore" hit home in more ways than one. Girls were mourning absent lovers, but that wasn't the only reason they weren't going out. The emergency Office

A generation of young adults put their personal lives on hold for the duration of the war. Paul J. Hartley (bottom, middle) and his wife, Kathleen (top), would later be Lowe's customers in Boone, North Carolina.

of Price Administration had been created, and automobile tires topped the list of items to be strictly rationed. Before the war was over, rationing would extend to bicycles, typewriters, stoves, shoes and galoshes, coffee, sugar, meats, fats, gasoline, fuel oil, and coal. Rationing was accompanied by a detailed program of price controls and other restrictions, some of which put limits on construction— including home building— for the duration of the war.

Ruth Lowe Buchan and her mother ran the hardware store as best they could in the constricted economy of the war years. They had to get used to shortages, to unreliable suppliers, to ration books, coupons, and stamps. They had to get used to telling people "No." It wasn't much fun— or very profitable. Like lots of businesses, Lowe's North Wilkesboro Hardware was just hanging on.

Then late in 1943, Carl Buchan suffered complications after a foot injury in Texas. He received an honorable discharge and came home. Unexpectedly free to pursue a normal life, ex-lieutenant Buchan needed a job. Jim Lowe, who was then based at Lowery Field in Colorado, made him an offer: take a complete inventory, pay me for a half interest, and we'll be partners.

Buchan later recalled taking inventory in the old store. "The stock consisted of notions, dry goods, horse collars, harnesses, snuff, produce, groceries, small miscellaneous hardware, and building materials," he wrote. It was all worth about $12,500. He didn't have that kind of money, but he knew where to get it. He went to Edwin Duncan, president of Northwestern Bank. Duncan hadn't gotten where he was by not knowing a good bet when it walked through the door. He lent Carl Buchan the money. It was, as Humphrey Bogart had said in *Casablanca*, "the start of a beautiful friendship."

On September 21, 1944, the "News And Views" column of the North Wilkesboro *Journal-Patriot* included the following item:

James L. Lowe, now a corporal in Uncle Sam's army, states that the two brick buildings he bought from I.H. McNeill last week, these being located on "C" street, will be used for expansion of the North Wilkesboro Hardware Co., which was established here by his father, the late L.S. Lowe.

Lowe's had its first expansion plan.

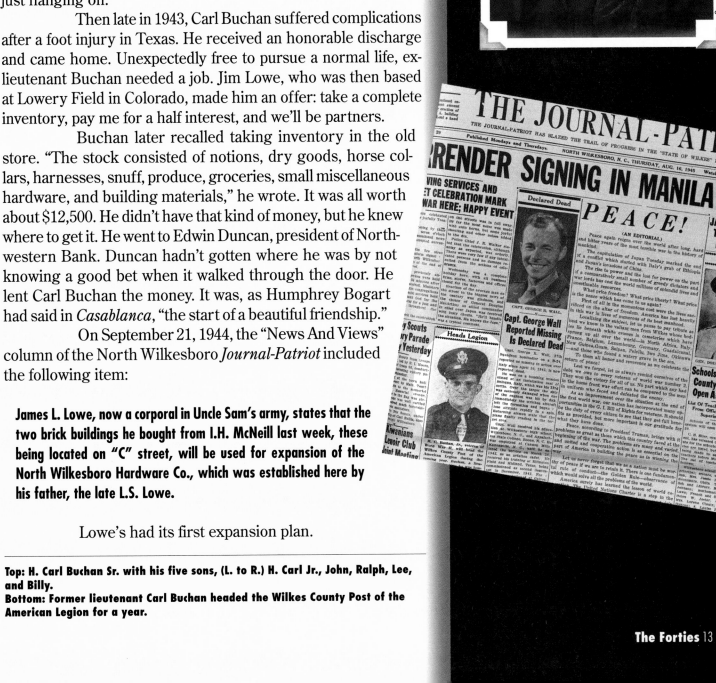

Top: H. Carl Buchan Sr. with his five sons, (L. to R.) H. Carl Jr., John, Ralph, Lee, and Billy.
Bottom: Former lieutenant Carl Buchan headed the Wilkes County Post of the American Legion for a year.

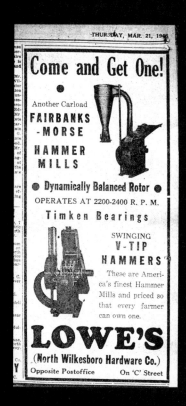

During the Depression, only five percent of all American households had an annual income greater than $4000. In 1945, the minimum hourly wage was still only 25 cents. You could buy a man's wool worsted suit at Penney's in North Wilkesboro for $25; a pair of work shoes in black elk ("Rationed free!") cost $2.98 at Belk's. A maple bedroom suite went for $47.50 at Forester Furniture. Shredded Wheat from the National Biscuit Company was 12 cents a box at the Dixie-Home Super Market. A year's subscription to the *Journal-Patriot* (okay, so it only came out twice a week) was $2.

In the *Journal-Patriot* you could find out if *The Corn Is Green*, starring Bette Davis, was still playing at the Allen. There were ads for custom-ground flour from Brier Creek Burr and Roller Mill, and for Dr. Kilmer's Swamp Root to relieve backache and that "run-down feeling". Lowe's Hardware didn't advertise heavily, but occasionally a manufacturer such as Fairbanks-Morse (maker of hammer mills "priced so that every farmer can own one") or Stag paints ("Stag Is the Leader In Wilkes County!") would offer to contribute to the cost of an ad.

On August 6, 1945, the atomic bomb was dropped on Hiroshima. On August 16, the *Journal-Patriot*'s headline read "SURRENDER SIGNING IN MANILA," followed by an editorial titled "Peace!" Just below, a captioned photograph of Carl Buchan in uniform announced that he would head the Wilkes County post of the American Legion for the coming year. It also identified him as "one of the city's most progressive young merchants." The city hadn't seen nothin' yet.

The one-two punch of the Depression and the war had sent the housing industry to the mat. Single-family housing starts had fallen from one million a year at the start of the period to just 114,000 in 1944. Now, with thousands of young men returning home, the housing shortage became a crisis. The apple tree was fine for sitting under, but it was no place to start a family. According to government estimates, more than five million new houses were needed immediately.

A housing bill sought to revive the building industry by means of federal mortgage guarantees that would protect home builders and thereby stimulate construction. Up on Long Island, a man named William Levitt took the incentive and ran with it. Levitt would soon gain renown— and be harshly criticized, as well— for his innovative response to the housing shortage. His system for mass-producing houses was based on Henry Ford's automotive assembly line. Giving top priority to quantity

---

Early Lowe's newspaper ads for paint and agricultural machines.

production rather than fine workmanship, Levitt found that maximum efficiency could be achieved by creating specialized teams of workers who performed their designated tasks and then moved on to the next site— which at Levittown was always nearby.

The basic Levitt Cape Cod bungalow sold for $7,990. It sat on a 60 x 100' lot and had a 12 x 16' living room, a kitchen, two bedrooms, and one bath. There were 17,000 of them at Levittown, offered to veterans (and soon to the public at large) with no required downpayment and no closing costs.

Bill Levitt bought appliances by the carload through wholly-owned Levitt subsidiaries. Smaller operators, including mom-and-pop retailers and traditional home builders, had to contend with backorders and high prices from manufacturers and wholesalers. Two decades of pent-up demand for all the basic components of a house resulted inevitably in shortages. Sourcing became an art form—one that Carl Buchan would master.

When Carl Buchan took over the management of Lowe's, he sold off everything except hardware and building materials. In the early postwar days of reconversion to a consumer economy, he realized that homeowners and home builders (individuals and professionals) would be good customers for any hard goods retailer who could provide a reliable supply of products at competitive prices. He resolved to make Lowe's just such a supplier.

Jim Lowe came home in March of 1946. For the first time, both partners were actively involved in the store. With Jim back on the scene, Carl had time to develop a network of sources, starting with some of the contacts he had made while working for the rail road. He began to acquire a reputation for getting things done.

A 1948 Lowe's invoice for plumbing fixtures and supplies.

In November of 1945, Major William H. McElwee returned to Wilkes County from service in the Judge Advocate General's Department of the U.S. Army in Europe. He reopened his law office at the Bank of North Wilkesboro; shortly thereafter, he became Carl Buchan's lawyer.

Brilliant and conservative, he would prove an important friend to Lowe's in trying times. When the company went public, he was made a founding director. He also served as a managing director and as Lowe's general counsel. In 1990, he became Lowe's first director emeritus.

"He had a mind like a steel trap," says Leonard Herring. "If I were in trouble and needed a trial lawyer, I'd rather have Bill McElwee than anyone else I've ever known."

Nearly a decade later, when young Leonard Herring was thinking of joining Lowe's, his father in Snow Hill spoke to a friend who owned a local hardware store. "There was a time when this man, Maynard Hicks, needed a load of asphalt and wasn't able to get it. Carl Buchan found it for him," Leonard says. "He told my father that Carl Buchan was a go-getter who was bound to be successful. Everybody said 'If you need something and you're having trouble getting it, call Carl Buchan!'"

Pete Kulynych recalls, "A lot of houses were built in the late Forties without commodes, because there was a real shortage. For years there had been no production for the consuming public. Everything was for the war. So commodes were scarce.

"If you were able to buy a load of commodes, it was just like hauling bootleg liquor: you sent an armed guard with 'em to keep them from being hijacked! Carl Buchan was able to get things like commodes when others couldn't."

As word spread about this aggressive little operation in North Wilkesboro, customers came from farther and farther afield. They brought trucks over tortuous mountain roads from Tennessee and West Virginia and Ohio. The train depot was only a few blocks down the hill from Lowe's, but so ferocious was the demand for goods that often a shipment arrived and was sold without a single door, window, or washing machine ever making it into the store. Pete would go down to the boxcar with Jim, Carl, or Hal Church, Lowe's first salesman. They did the dickering; he would take the cash as fast as customers could thrust it at him.

If there was something that a customer needed, Buchan wanted Lowe's to provide it. According to Pete, he used to say "We've got to pay attention to what kind of people our customers are. If we've got a fellow with a truck from Missouri who's building his house, he needs furniture. Why can't we put a bedroom suite on his truck— and a mattress?" So Lowe's sold furniture and mattresses.

Buchan said "People come here on tires; why don't we sell them tires?" So Lowe's sold tires and even owned a re-capping service for a while, although that experiment was ultimately deemed a failure. Pete explains, "We sold the tires on time payment, and some of those boys would wear 'em out over the weekend. Then they didn't want to pay for them."

As the hardware thrived, the partners put some of the profits into other joint ventures. They started B&L Motors, a Cadillac and Oldsmobile dealership; they also bought a farm together just over the mountain in Alleghany County, and stocked it with white-face Hereford cattle.

It was the purchase of that farm, called Scenic Valley, that stimulated the pair's interest in the nearby town of Sparta—and particularly in Sparta Farm Supply, a feed-and-seed owned by a man named Clinton Halsey. Carl Buchan and Jim Lowe started buying their farm supplies from him. Before long, it occurred to them that a Lowe's store on this side of the Blue Ridge would enable lots of people to buy from Lowe's without having to cross the mountains. Pete remembers that they deputized Hal Church to negotiate the deal, because Mr. Halsey didn't approve of the brash young owners of Lowe's.

Edith Richardson supported herself and her young son on her income as Clinton Halsey's secretary and bookkeeper. "The store was a cinder block building with a pot-bellied stove and a hand-cranked cash register in the office," she says. "You could ring up $99.99 on it, but if the sale was bigger than that, you had to ring it up in increments."

The first time she met Carl Buchan and Jim Lowe, Edith recalls, "It was cold, so they came in wearing heavy jackets and looking just like ordinary customers. By then Mr. Halsey knew who was behind the deal, and he was resigned to it. I was excited because he told me they were ambitious and growing, and I thought we would do better. They both seemed like men who wanted to go places and get things done."

They installed a manager and got rid of the feed and the other purely agricultural supplies. They stuffed the little store full of building materials, hardware, and appliances, until the warehouse overflowed and they had to stack some of the plumbing supplies outside. They called it Lowe's Sparta Hardware Store.

Jim Lowe was satisfied: this was all the hardware stores he ever expected to need. But Carl Buchan was beginning to dream of Lowe's stores in a chain that would one day reach from sea to shining sea.

- - -

Lowe's store #2 opened in Sparta, North Carolina (population 800) in 1949.

The Fifties

Voices

"In my employment interview, Cecil Huskey asked me what was the least I could live on. Unfortunately, I told him. And that's what I came to work at Lowe's for."

— Mike Brown

"One time Carl Buchan came back to the receiving area in the Roanoke store and he saw some leftover ends of pipe that we had cut for a customer. 'Get that cleaned up,' he told me. I said "Yes sir, I'll get it cleaned up for you.' 'Not for me,' he corrected. 'Do it for yourself.'"

— Kyle McNeil

"Pete Kulynych's desk was a door laid over two kegs, and he had two nails— one for paid bills, one for unpaid bills."

— Ed Beach

"I had asked them to take me to the warehouse on the day of my interview. There were steel lintels, and rolls of barbed wire, and mountains of nails in kegs from Czechoslovakia, and it was all interesting to me."

— Richard Hauser

"Sometimes before we took inventory, Jim Lowe would walk through a store with an old scratch pad. Then he would write down a figure and lock it in the safe. We'd take the inventory and match it against his guess. It was uncanny how close he'd be, every time."

— Pete Kulynych

"I was interviewed by Carl Buchan on a Sunday. He was chain-smoking Camels, and we talked about this and that, and suddenly he slapped his hand on the table and said 'How much do you want to make?' I said 'Gosh, I don't think I'd put a ceiling on it.' And he said 'That's the right damn answer! Come to work tomorrow morning.'"

— Bob Gresham

"I didn't mind going to work of a morning, because you were getting somewhere."

— Edith Richardson

"My sales training at the Sparta store consisted of Bill Sebastian taking me to the cash register and handing me some invoice forms and saying 'Get out there and wait on some of these people.'"

— B.J. Bare

"I think there were seven or eight of us store managers around the table. Carl Buchan said, 'Men, I've got good news and bad news. The good news is, I've bought eight truckloads of roofing. The bad news is, I don't have the money to pay for it. So it had better be sold before the invoice comes due.' And every bundle of that roofing was sold."

— Ross Burgess

"He said 'I want you to start an airline for me, because I'm gonna build a nationwide chain of stores, and I'm gonna keep the headquarters right here in North Wilkesboro. I want to use airplanes. And before I'm done, you'll be flying jets.'"

— Max Freeman

"It takes big plans to do big things."

— Carl Buchan

Lowe's was looking for a few good men. When Carl Buchan went to King's Business College in search of a bookkeeper, he specifically asked for male applicants. After all, the building supply and hardware industry was a man's world. The merchandise was big and heavy, marketed with an emphasis on function over fashion. It was made by men, sold to men, and used (or at least installed) by men.

Although eight million women had joined the national work force during the war, many filling jobs in heavy industry, the postwar years quickly reversed that trend. Rosie the Riveter had been a patriotic necessity; the postwar ideal was more like Betty Crocker. A woman's place was not on Lowe's loading dock, and it would be years before women would be recruited for any jobs at Lowe's that a man could do.

Gladieux Family Collection

During the Christmas shopping season of 1949, Wiley McNeil was working in the men's department at Belk's in North Wilkesboro. Carl Buchan was hiring, and he heard that Belk's had a good salesman who might be ready for a change. Buchan sent Hal Church to buy a shirt from this McNeil fellow and invite him for an interview.

Unfortunately, there was another McNeil working on the sales floor that day, and he told Church that there was no way he would leave Belk's for "that little two-story hardware store." The next day, Wiley recalls, "Hal Church came back to buy another shirt. This time he got the right McNeil. So I went to see Carl Buchan, and he offered me $45 a week. In January of 1950, I started working for Lowe's."

By now, Pete Kulynych not only managed the books, he also kept track of inventory and did some purchasing. Carl Buchan made buying trips to New York and Philadelphia, among other places, in pursuit of good deals. Jim Lowe stayed closer to home, dividing his time and attention among his various enterprises. Wiley McNeil and Hal Church alternated opening

Top: In the Fifties, WWII veterans who went to college on the G.I. Bill looked for secure jobs with large companies, started families, and bought houses in the suburbs.

Bottom: On a single income, a family could afford a house, a car, and all the latest appliances, take an annual vacation, and have two or three children. (And, in some cases, a horse.)

Hartley Family Collection

and closing the North Wilkesboro store and keeping the floors swept.

Lowe's salesmen were free to dicker in order to make a sale. "We had stacks of cost cards, one card for each item," says Wiley. "As long as we got ten percent over Lowe's cost, we were doing okay."

Bob Gresham, who joined Lowe's in 1951, says "Carl Buchan would get on us quicker for overcharging than for undercharging. He wanted us always to make the sale. He would say 'I'd rather have three customers and make ten percent from each of them than to have just one customer and make thirty percent.' He was a genius at building a customer franchise."

Carl Buchan's salesmanship was rational and highly evolved compared with his partner's instinctive wheeler-dealer style. Jim Lowe was a hearty, happy-go-lucky guy whose large frame had inspired the nickname "Puny." He had been in retailing all his life: he was practically born in the family store, and from the age of twelve he helped his father make deliveries. In 1946, home from the Pacific, he met and fell in love with dark-haired Lucy Thurston, a teacher from Taylorsville. In February of 1947 they married, and for a while they lived with Jim's mother in the old house on Trogdon Street where Jim had grown up.

They had two sons together, and the marriage endured, but nobody who knew Jim Lowe was surprised

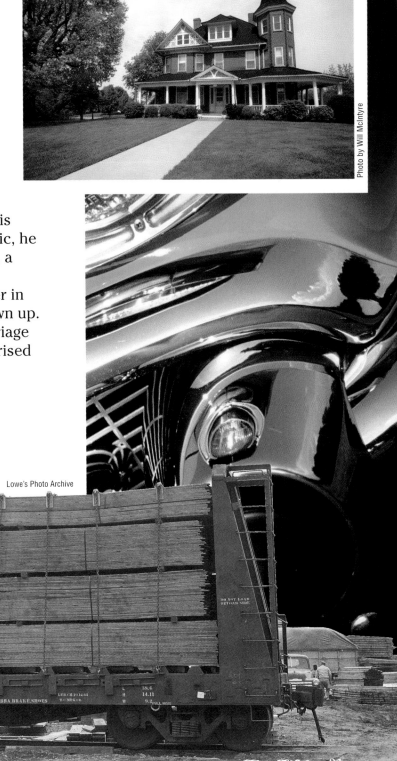

Top: The Lowe family home on Trogdon Street in North Wilkesboro.
Bottom: Billy Bare and Hal Church atop a rail car loaded with lumber. For shipping convenience, Lowe's early stores were located close to railway sidings.

Lowe's Photo Archive

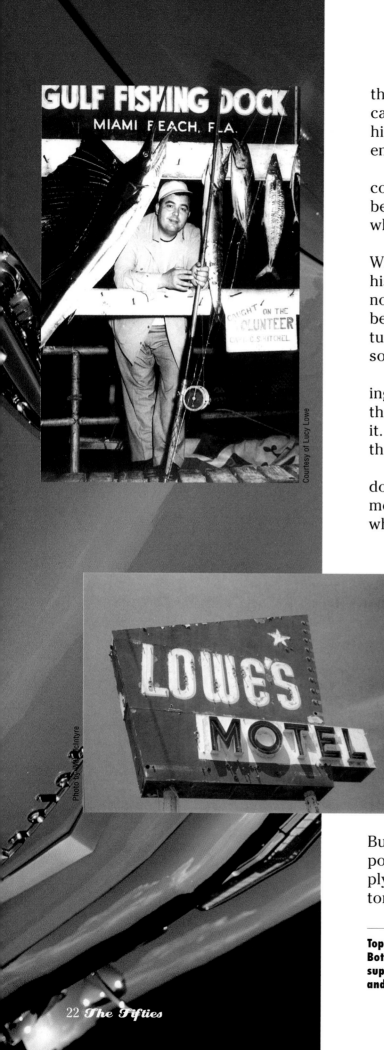

Courtesy of Lucy Lowe

Photo by Mike McIntyre

that he didn't live to be an octogenarian. He burned his candle at both ends, and his unbridled enthusiasms got him into more ventures and adventures than most lives encompass in a much longer span.

"Jim was a salesman," says Pete Kulynych. "He could sell a refrigerator to a penguin. The difference between Carl and Jim was that Carl thought long-range, whereas Jim was a short-timer."

He was also a lifelong resident of North Wilkesboro who was perfectly content to be a big fish in his hometown pond. Carl Buchan, on the other hand, saw no reason why Lowe's marketplace shouldn't extend far beyond its current perimeter. By 1952, he had his opportunistic eye on the city of Asheville, one hundred miles southwest along the Blue Ridge in Buncombe County.

"There was a place selling millwork and building materials on Biltmore Avenue in Asheville, down near the Vanderbilt estate," Pete recalls. "Carl wanted to buy it. So he and Jim went over there and made the deal, and they were each to put up half the money.

"Well, on the morning of the closing, Jim came down to the office and said he wasn't going to take his money out of town. So the deal fell through. And that's when negotiations began for Carl and Jim to separate."

Jay Grisette was a young accountant whose firm had been doing work for Lowe's since 1947. With help from him and attorney Bill McElwee, as well as Ed Duncan at Northwestern Bank, the nine-year partnership was brought to an amicable end. Jim Lowe took B&L Motors and the cattle farm, which he would later sell back to his brother-in-law. Carl Buchan became the sole owner of Lowe's.

Buchan immediately renewed contact with Asheville. In October of 1952, the building on Biltmore Avenue became Lowe's Asheville Hardware Store. Its manager was the former Belk's clerk, Wiley McNeil.

Because tax laws exempted the first $25,000 of every corporation's annual profits, Carl Buchan decided that each Lowe's store should be incorporated individually under the umbrella of Buchan Supply Company. A corporation needed directors, and directors had to be shareholders, so Buchan would invite key

Top: Jim Lowe at play with the catch of the day in Florida.
Bottom: Jim Lowe's ventures after splitting with Carl Buchan included a supermarket (which became Lowe's Foods), a bowling alley, a skating rink, and Lowe's Motel.

employees to be directors with him, giving them one share of stock in exchange for their signatures on the incorporation documents. In this way, Pete and Hal Church and a handful of others became early shareholders of Lowe's. At the time, the shares were mere tokens; later, they would become extremely important.

Pete was beginning to feel that he might be a part of something big. Business was good: Lowe's was earning a reputation for selling name brand merchandise at the lowest prices around. Postwar shortages were largely a thing of the past. These days, Carl Buchan's ingenuity was focused on making Lowe's a soup-to-nuts source for all the products needed to build a home. This had never been attempted under one retailer's roof. Adding even more daring to the endeavor, he adopted a controversial sourcing strategy summed up by the letters "DTU."

Direct To User: the phrase represented a rebellion against wholesalers and other middlemen in the standard distribution networks of that time. For years, manufacturers had guaranteed their independent distributors that they would be protected from competition within their territories. As better highways and communications systems changed the way goods were bought, shipped, and warehoused, the system became outmoded. Now it wasn't unusual for the distributor to get a piece of the action on products he had never seen or touched.

"We would buy a carload of roofing from a salesman," Pete says, "but the bill would come from a jobber. And the sucker didn't do anything except make our cost higher!"

It infuriated Carl Buchan that anybody should make money without adding value to a product, especially when it meant that manufacturers refused to sell to Lowe's.

"We had a hard time getting bathtubs, because American Standard only dealt with wholesalers," Pete recalls. "Kohler wouldn't let us in the door. See, plumbers bought everything from wholesalers. Electricians bought

Collection of Mike Brown

Photo by Will McIntyre

Top: Store #3, Lowe's Asheville Hardware on Biltmore Avenue.
Middle: In 1954, Jake and Mamie Lee Wilson of Vale, NC drove fifty miles to Lowe's in North Wilkesboro to furnish their home. Their kitchen still has many of the original features (and Mamie still has her nightgown from their wedding night).
Bottom: A 1951 Chevrolet Club Coupe.

Gladieux Family Collection

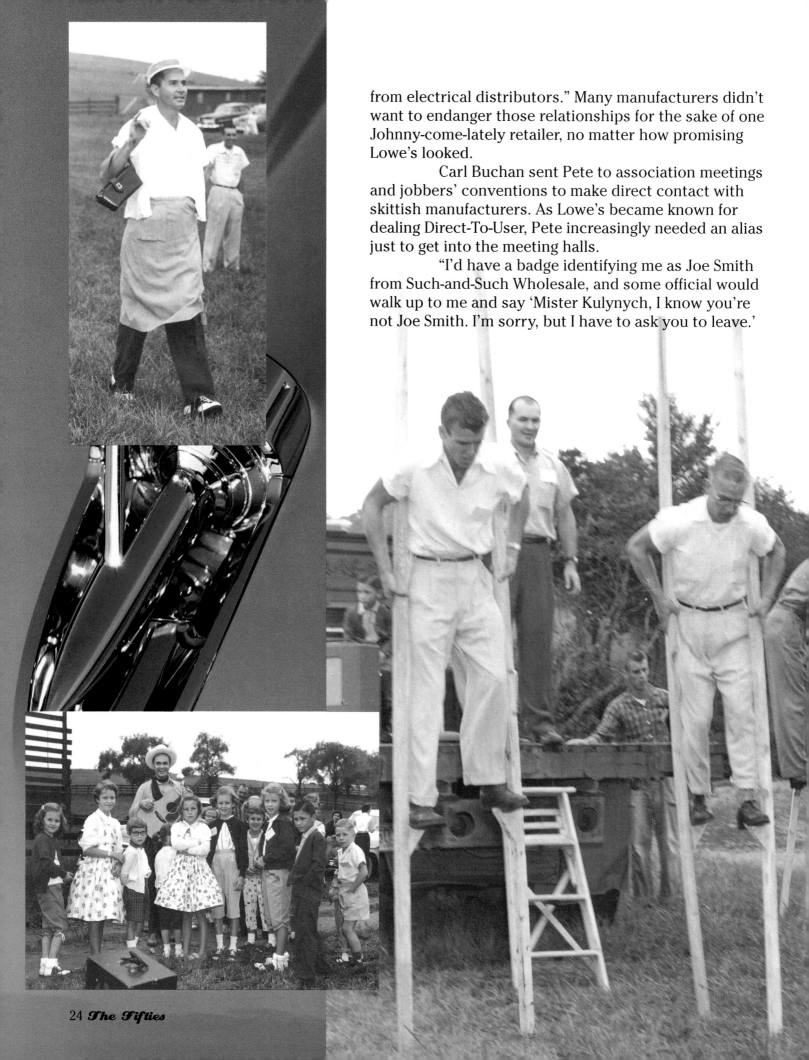

from electrical distributors." Many manufacturers didn't want to endanger those relationships for the sake of one Johnny-come-lately retailer, no matter how promising Lowe's looked.

Carl Buchan sent Pete to association meetings and jobbers' conventions to make direct contact with skittish manufacturers. As Lowe's became known for dealing Direct-To-User, Pete increasingly needed an alias just to get into the meeting halls.

"I'd have a badge identifying me as Joe Smith from Such-and-Such Wholesale, and some official would walk up to me and say 'Mister Kulynych, I know you're not Joe Smith. I'm sorry, but I have to ask you to leave.'

I'll bet I was kicked out of more of those things than anybody in the country.

"One day the rep for Möen [plumbing products] came to see me. Möen is a good line, and we were doing good business directly with the company. He was very apologetic, but he said 'We just can't sell to you anymore.'"

Lowe's resourcefulness in finding alternative suppliers gradually chipped away at the walls of resistance, although it would be years before they crumbled. In the meantime, Lowe's would make itself harder for suppliers to ignore by building impressive sales to the booming new do-it-yourself (DIY) industry.

Early American settlers had no choice but to do-it-themselves. Over time, their "know-how" and "can-do" acquired a patriotic glow and became part of our

Photos these pages courtesy of Nancy Canter

After Carl Buchan bought it back from Jim Lowe, the Scenic Valley farm was the site of company picnics and Fourth of July barbecues. Taken at a 1958 celebration, these photos show: Hal Church wearing a skirt and bonnet and carrying a purse; entertainer Fred Kirby of WBTV, Charlotte, with young audience members; Pete Kulynych (on truck) officiating a stilt race; and Mary Elizabeth Buchan, eight years old, addressing the gathering under her father's watchful eye.

national self-image. In the years after World War II, seven million Americans became new homeowners— and weekend plumbers, woodworkers, and decorators. Home workshops proliferated in garages and basements. Home improvement attained the status of a national hobby and was practiced even by celebrities such as Perry Como, Desi Arnaz, and Jane Russell.

The cover story for the August 2, 1954 issue of *Time* celebrated the DIY phenomenon, partly crediting the trend to the war itself:

*D*uring their service years, millions of Americans learned for the first time how to repair radios, engines and dozens of other machines. Housewives who had been punch-press operators, welders and electronics technicians found that it was no trick to fix a leaky faucet or paper a room, especially as it was hard to hire anyone to do it. Doing it herself was also less expensive, since the wages of carpenters and plumbers had jumped far higher than those of many other workers.

The article revealed that in 1953, amateur decorators "slapped on" 75% of all the paint sold nationally. They also hung 60% of the wallpaper and laid 50% of the asphalt tile ("enough to cover the entire state of Oregon").

Keenly aware of the trend, Carl Buchan was determined to make Lowe's the first choice of America's bargain-hunting do-it-yourselfers. To do that, he would keep costs trimmed to the bone while building Lowe's purchasing clout. Increased sales volume would help, and that would come with expansion. In February of 1954, he opened Lowe's Asheboro Hardware. It was followed in June of 1955 by Lowe's Charlotte Hardware, and in November by Lowe's Durham Hardware. Lowe's now had six stores.

Early on, Carl Buchan had a feeling for technology's potential in inventory management. He bought two IBM model 402 computers, and he hired Clint Packard from Hennis Motor Lines in Winston-Salem to be Lowe's first data processing expert and branch inventory manager.

One Saturday morning, Packard sent a truck from C&S Motor Freight in North Wilkesboro over to the

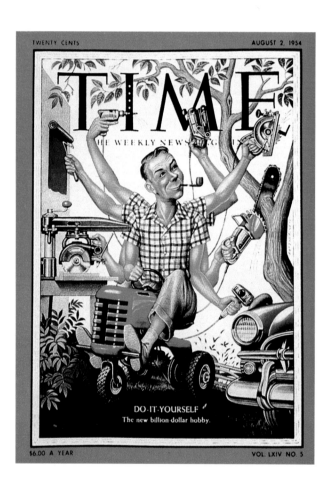

The August 2, 1954 issue of *Time* featured the Do-It-Yourself phenomenon. ©1954 Time Magazine. Reprinted with permission.

Asheville store with a load of merchandise. Says Wiley McNeil, "We were so busy all day, we couldn't find time to unload the truck. Late in the afternoon, Clint Packard called me and fired me. I got in touch with Carl Buchan, because he had told me never to let anything get in the way of a sale.

"Mr. Buchan called me on Sunday evening and said 'You go back to that store tomorrow and keep doing what you've been doing.'"

By October of 1955, Lowe's was in the market for a new data processing expert. Carl Buchan asked Pete Kulynych to place a classified ad in newspapers around the region. One of the responses came from a self-taught data processing manager who was working for a textile concern called Stonecutter Mills.

Joe Reinhardt was a mild-mannered young man with a taste for practical jokes and a passion for automobiles and motorcycles. He was looking for a change, and he found Carl Buchan's energy and conviction infectious. In January of 1956, he signed on as Lowe's IBM manager.

Along with the ad that brought Joe Reinhardt to Lowe's, Pete had placed one for an office manager and accountant. It ran in the *News and Observer* of Raleigh, and was seen by a Chapel Hill alumnus who was managing the office of H. Weil and Brothers in Goldsboro.

Leonard Herring had received his bachelor's degree in commerce in 1948 and been recruited by Dun and Bradstreet to travel the Carolinas reporting on a variety of businesses from textile mills to rural grocery stores. The job had taken him to Wilson, where he had met his wife, Rose. It had also taken him to Goldsboro and put him within the gravitational field of Henry Weil.

The Weil family was both prominent and Jewish, which was unusual for a small town in eastern North Carolina. They had operated a department store in Goldsboro for a

Top: In the 1950's, everything in America was booming, including the birthrate. Even on TV, people were having babies: Lucille Ball's televised pregnancy in 1952 coincided with the national trend.
Bottom: Americans were increasingly mobile and lived farther from their workplaces than ever before. Charles Eckman, Jr. of Bloomington, Indiana stands with his Oldsmobile 88 on Thanksgiving Day, 1955.

Courtesy of Building Supply News

hundred years. They also owned a lot of farm land and a fertilizer mixing plant. Their company was a family affair, but Henry Weil was impressed by the young rep from Dun and Bradstreet, and he offered him a job. Leonard Herring was flattered, intrigued— and ready to stop traveling. He accepted, and entered the world of retailing.

He stayed with Henry Weil for six years. Finally, though, he realized that since his name wasn't Weil, there was a limit to how much he could do there. Two of the partners had sons who would soon be graduating from college and entering the family business. Then Leonard saw the Lowe's ad in the Raleigh newspaper, and decided to submit his resumé.

Pete later told Leonard that the response to the ad was overwhelming: he said he must have received several hundred applications. But Pete and Carl invited Leonard Herring to North Wilkesboro for an interview.

It was a small world. When Carl Buchan was working for the Atlantic and East Coast Rail Road, there had been a director named Frank Seymour who was also a partner in Weil's. Based on his knowledge of Frank Seymour and Weil's, Carl thought that if this Leonard Herring had been at Weil's for six years, he must have something going for him. It was all Carl Buchan needed to confirm his own inclination. In December of 1955, Leonard Herring joined Lowe's as its first financial officer.

The late Fifties were building years for Lowe's. In 1957, the chain opened three stores: at the time, it was a fifty percent expansion. The Greensboro store went into an existing facility, but the stores in Winston-Salem and Roanoke were custom-built for Lowe's.

In a speech at the end of the decade, Carl Buchan would declare with pride that "During all of this growth period, it has not been necessary to borrow one dime of outside capital." Although he was the best of friends with Ed Duncan,

**Top: Joe Reinhardt extolls the virtues of 1950's computer technology.
Bottom: Leonard and Rose Herring in the backyard of the Herring home place in Snow Hill, North Carolina in the summer of 1951.**

whose Northwestern Bank had become a regional power-house, Buchan didn't want to sell anybody the power to control his business. "As far as I'm concerned," he said, "a non-productive stockholder is an unnecessary evil." The only exception he ever made was for Winston-Salem businessman Robert Hanes, with whom he served on the State Board of Conservation and Development. Robert Hanes was invited to buy a partial interest in two Lowe's stores.

Instead of borrowing from banks, Buchan developed an approach to funding which gave employees a stake in the company and may have planted the seeds for what was to come. He sold 49% of his interest in the Durham and Roanoke stores to Lowe's employees, who bought in through a combination loan and stock purchase.

Leonard explains, "It worked like this: for $11, you purchased a $1 share of stock and you made a $10 loan to the store. So most of what you put out was a loan that the store was obligated to pay back, while a small part paid for the stock. Most people couldn't buy much, but even a few shares converted to big bucks down the road.

"I wasn't with Lowe's when the Durham store was funded, but for the Roanoke store I put up everything I had. I borrowed $7200, which was a lot of money back then."

It wasn't just Lowe's management who participated. Edith Richardson had moved to the Charlotte store by then, but she went back to her former boss at Sparta Farm Supply for a loan to buy stock in the Durham Lowe's store.

"We could put in $5000," she recalls. "It was like a bond: the store would start paying it back, and every time I received a payment, I made a payment on what I had borrowed." Edith became one of Lowe's early financial success stories.

You might say Lowe's got Bob Strickland as a Green Stamp premium. In the summer of 1956, the young Asheboro native was hired by one of his professors at Harvard Business School to help with a market analysis

Lowe's Greensboro Hardware opened in 1957 with 4,000 square feet of sales floor and a 38,000-square-foot warehouse.

Lowe's Aviation

When Max Freeman graduated from "The West Point of the Air" in 1942, the Air Force Academy was so new that its name hadn't even been established. His class called itself "42-X," because "X" commonly identified experiments in aviation!

Max became a captain in the Army Air Corps, flying B-29 bombers out of Hunter AFB in Savannah and taking KB-29 tankers from Havana to Boston. After the war, he flew military surplus planes part-time out of the airport at Hickory, NC, then worked his way down to Miami and back, landing in Shelby in 1948.

"I was teaching G.I. Bill veterans how to fly," he recalls, "and this fellow came in fresh from a hitch as a deckhand on a Navy carrier. It was Norm Robbins." Max taught him to fly, and would later hire him for Lowe's. When Max retired, Norm became Lowe's chief pilot.

In 1958, Max heard that Lowe's was looking for a plane and a pilot. He flew up to North Wilkesboro in a Cessna 182 and Pete Kulynych agreed to buy it for the company. The following Saturday, when Max came to the general office to pick up his check, Carl Buchan persuaded him to work for Lowe's full time.

Back then, the North Wilkesboro airport was a dirt strip in a cow pasture. But as usual, Carl Buchan was thinking big. He said, "There are people working here who are scoutmasters, who sing in church choirs, who are active in civic things, and I want them to be home at the end of the workday. Your job is to get 'em back home.

"I always want to have an airplane that will keep them within two flying hours of home base. That means that someday, when you're working for Lowe's a thousand miles from here, you'll be flying 500-mph jets."

"And that's the way it happened," says Max.

commissioned by Sperry and Hutchinson Green Stamp Company. His job was to survey retailers in the Carolinas and Virginia to determine the effectiveness of green stamps in each market.

"I went into an appliance store in Durham," Bob recalls, "and I asked him if green stamps helped his business. He said 'Not anymore. Business hasn't been good since Lowe's came to town. They're selling Hotpoint appliances to customers for just about what my cost is.'"

Bob decided he'd better check out Lowe's operation. "I went to Lowe's of Durham, and they had these stand-up sales desks at the back of the store. I fell in line and finally got up to the counter. Al Plemmons was the salesman; he was paid on commission, as all salesmen were then.

"I had my paperwork out, and I began my spiel about how 'I'm here to do a survey—,' and Al looked over my shoulder at all the people standing in line to buy something and increase his commission, and he said 'We're not allowed to talk about things like that. You'll have to go up to North Wilkesboro.' That was my first exposure to Lowe's."

He went back to Harvard to start his second year, and to his surprise saw a notice for "Lowe's of North Carolina" among the postings for possible job interviews. Leonard Herring came to Cambridge with Cecil Huskey, whom Carl Buchan had hired from United Fruit Company to be Lowe's director of operations. They invited the young MBA candidate to North Wilkesboro for a visit.

"I came down from Cambridge one Saturday, and the first thing I saw, across the street from Lowe's, was a street preacher waving his arms in front of the Red Cross Pharmacy.

"Pete was in the office, and he had his desk covered with rail schedules, trying to figure out how to ship sheet rock into Galax by rail and truck it down to North Wilkesboro to save money. I was impressed with his work ethic.

"Then I met Carl Buchan. He was very intense, short-spoken, obviously driven. I knew he was on to something. He had a vision of Lowe's as a national chain, and he said 'I want you to be part of it.'"

When Bob got back to Cambridge, he told his wife, Betty, that if he were single he would probably take

Courtesy of Geraldine Bumgarner

Geraldine Bumgarner makes an attractive hood ornament on a 1955 Chevy. She would join Lowe's in 1963.

Lowe's Photo Archive

the Lowe's job. Since their wedding in 1952, the couple had lived in San Francisco, Norfolk, and Boston. Lately they had been planning and looking forward to a move to Manhattan, where Bob had been offered a job with the legendary ad agency Young and Rubicam.

Now Betty said, "It shouldn't matter whether you're married or single; you should take the best job." "Okay," Bob decided, "Let's try Lowe's for two years."

Before joining Lowe's as a manager trainee in June of 1957, he went back for a second visit. This time, Carl Buchan took him on a tour of the new store that had replaced the old C Street hardware. The new store had a 3,000-square-foot sales floor and a cavernous 40,000-square-foot warehouse. The store manager escorted Carl and Bob through the warehouse. Deep in one corner was a neglected-looking pile of miscellaneous merchandise.

"Carl Buchan asked the manager 'What is that?'" Bob Strickland recalls. 'It's damaged merchandise, Mr. Buchan,' the manager answered. Buchan said, 'Look a little closer and tell me what you see.' 'Um, I see a water pump, some broken windows, and some dented guttering.'

"'That's what you see?' Carl Buchan persisted. 'Yes, sir.' By now, the manager's eyes were getting big, because he knew something was up. Then Buchan said, 'That's not what I see. What I see over there is my money: I paid for all that. And before long, we'll have a program in place so that when you look over there, you'll see *your* money, too. And when you see *your* money there, you'll take better care of it.'"

*L*owe's Profit-Sharing Plan and Trust was established in June of 1957. From then on, employees who made a real commitment to Lowe's would receive a real reward *from* Lowe's— a share in the fruits of their own labors, something which traditionally went without apology to capitalists, not to worker bees.

The idea for a profit-sharing plan had been gestating in Carl Buchan's mind at least since Leonard Herring signed on in December of 1955. Lowe's already had a pension plan, but as Carl told Leonard, "On this pension plan, people don't get their money until they're

The new North Wilkesboro store on Highway 268 East replaced the C Street store in 1957.

fifty or sixty years old. I've got lots of people who are thirty, and they couldn't care less about a pension plan. I want a profit-sharing plan so I can send 'em a statement every year and let them see that they're getting somewhere."

Carl Buchan's interest in profit-sharing was not philanthropic. He was a self-taught behavioral scientist: his theory, based on observation, was that people would work harder if they felt they were working for themselves— in other words, if they had a stake in Lowe's profitability.

Leonard had learned about profit-sharing plans back in Goldsboro at Weil's. Henry Weil had set up a plan in 1942; when Leonard came to Lowe's, he brought an understanding of the mechanics of profit-sharing and a willingness to adapt the Weil's model to suit Lowe's needs. The drafting of a plan was an early topic of conversation between him and Carl Buchan, and one on which he was happy to follow through. When the plan was instituted, Leonard became its trustee. He would continue in that role for more than twenty years.

In addition to its incentive function, the profit-sharing plan was important to Carl Buchan for another reason. He was planning for posterity, setting up his estate. He wanted to give the profit-sharing plan an option to buy a certain amount of Lowe's stock from him every year, and the balance at his death. In this way he would provide for the welfare of his wife, Ruth, and their daughter, Mary Elizabeth. He would also ensure that Lowe's would belong to those who built it, and who had its best interests at heart.

Carl Buchan also bought roughly two million dollars of life insurance. Leonard explains, "He knew he had all this stock but no cash of any consequence. If he died and his stock was taken for taxes, his estate wouldn't have enough money to buy it clear. The life insurance was made payable to the company, so that the company could pay his estate taxes and redeem his stock.

"That's very far-seeing for a man in his early forties, but remember: this was a man who also foresaw a little southern hardware store becoming a national company."

Carl Buchan's foresight may have had another explanation, too. He was the oldest of five brothers whose mother had died young. Although just a couple of years older than his nearest sibling, he showed an almost paternal concern for the welfare of the four younger

Courtesy of Betty Strickland

boys. Billy, the youngest, was nine years his junior. While a student at UNC-Chapel Hill, Billy was managing editor of *The Daily Tarheel*. He became a journalist and went to work for a newspaper in Jacksonville, North Carolina. Carl, who had once planned a career in journalism for himself, was proud of Billy. But at the age of twenty-seven, Billy Buchan suffered a massive heart attack and died on the job.

To all appearances, Carl Buchan was hale and hearty at forty. The physical disability that got him an early discharge from military service was related to bones in his feet. But what could alert you to mortality more effectively than to have your baby brother die of a heart attack at twenty-seven?

Carl Buchan was a long-range planner. He also recognized the need to delegate authority—a rare quality in an entrepreneur.

"Most entrepreneurs think they always have to do everything themselves, because in the beginning, they probably did!" says Leonard Herring. "Carl Buchan wasn't like that. He knew that if Lowe's was going to be a national company, he had to trust his people to run it."

Bob Strickland had come to Lowe's expecting to be made manager of the Greensboro store. Then the advertising manager at the general office was fired, and Bob was told that Cecil Huskey wanted him in North Wilkesboro.

"So I took over as ad manager, reporting to Cecil Huskey and working with an agency called Bennett Advertising," Bob says.

He walked right into the middle of the Sunbeam case. Pete Kulynych had purchased some appliances from Sunbeam, and Cecil Huskey decided to promote them at a price lower than the manufacturer's retail minimum. Sunbeam sued.

"There was a thing called a Fair Trade Law on the books in North Carolina," Pete explains. "If you bought from a manufacturer, you had to sign their pricing agreement. Then you couldn't advertise their products for sale below their designated price."

It was all part of the system of protected distribution which Lowe's was tackling head-on. Companies didn't want Lowe's selling below their minimum retail prices, because their smaller dealers would accuse them of giving Lowe's special deals for buying in quantity.

Bob Strickland told Betty that he wanted to try Lowe's for two years.

Lowe's was indeed buying in quantity, while keeping operating costs low: the final ingredient for profitability was the high sales volume which Lowe's Low Prices would deliver.

The differences were irreconcilable, and the case went to U.S. District Court in Newton. As Lowe's vice president of purchasing, Pete accompanied Bill McElwee to defend Cecil Huskey's pricing decision.

Pete later told Bob Strickland, "The Sunbeam plane landed, and six lawyers got out wearing homburgs and chesterfields, and every damn one of them looked like John Foster Dulles!"

Sunbeam asked Judge Warlick for an injunction to make Lowe's stop selling their appliances below the minimum price. They presented the ad which had started the dispute. According to Pete, "The judge said 'It looks like I'm going to have to grant this injunction. Maybe I ought to call my wife and see if we need a toaster or anything from Lowe's before I put it into effect!'"

Lowe's was prevented from selling Sunbeam's appliances at the price that had been advertised. Sunbeam took back the goods and refunded Lowe's money. The whole affair was costly, but Bob Strickland made the best of it. "We lost, and it cost," he wrote in one follow-up advertisement. "We're just sorry that we weren't successful in our attempt to save more money for our customers."

It wasn't long before General Electric led the way in abandoning the Fair Trade Laws. Other manufacturers, including Sunbeam, followed suit. But the expense and wasted energy of the Sunbeam case drove a wedge between Cecil Huskey and Carl Buchan. Ultimately, Huskey was fired.

"Buchan called me," Bob Strickland remembers. "He said 'Huskey's gotta go. I've been watching you work for a few months now, and I want you to hold down his job for a while. There's a guy named Walker that I'm trying to hire, but in the meantime, you keep advertising and promotion.' So that's what I did."

The "guy named Walker" was a born salesman, a regional manager for Hotpoint whose territory had included Lowe's until he was transferred to Chicago in 1956. When Johnny Walker came to Lowe's to conduct sales meetings for Hotpoint, even secretaries and warehousemen got excited about selling refrigerators. Carl Buchan was impressed, and made repeated overtures. In 1956, Walker turned him down because he wanted the

These ads followed the resolution of the Sunbeam Fair Trade lawsuit.

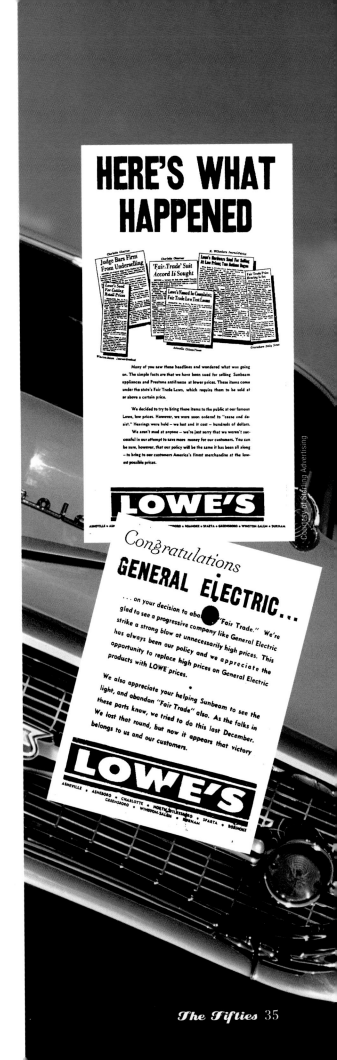

Lowe's Photo Archive

Lowe's Photo Archive

Lowe's Photo Archive

Chicago experience. But in 1958, when Hotpoint tried to move Johnny to California, he decided it was time to accept Buchan's latest offer. He joined Lowe's in March of 1958 as sales manager with additional responsibility for merchandising, promotions, and branch managers. He was Lowe's 344th employee.

There had never been anyone like Johnny Walker at Lowe's. Leonard Herring remembers being called into Carl Buchan's office along with Pete, around the time of Johnny's arrival. "Carl knew that he had a solid base. What he needed was a zip man, and that's what he got in Walker. He told us, 'I need you to follow up behind him and keep things straight.'

"Carl Buchan was a genius at empowerment and control. He would empower people to do something, then put in controls to make sure it would get done right."

*W*ith the addition of Johnny Walker, Buchan felt he had a core of leadership that could take Lowe's anywhere he wanted it to go. One day they were all eating lunch at his sprawling brick house on Finley Avenue. He leaned back in his seat and looked around the table at the five young executives— Pete, Leonard, Joe, Bob, and Johnny— and remarked with satisfaction, "Well, I've got my team together."

Lowe's continued to grow. In 1958, Lowe's stores opened in Chester, South Carolina; Raleigh, North Carolina; and Knoxville, Tennessee. They would be followed by several more in 1959.

The Knoxville store became especially important as the crucible for a major strategic shift. John Walker, whose background was in wholesale, believed that Lowe's primary customer franchise should be big-ticket professional building contractors rather than homeowners. Knoxville was Lowe's largest market at the time, so it was there that Walker chose to court contractors by extending them credit and offering free delivery to construction sites. Sales soared, and the emphasis on contractor customers would dominate Lowe's for the next fifteen years.

In March of 1959, more than a hundred manufacturers received invitations to a dinner program in Charlotte called "Lowe's Golden Opportunity Year." Presentations were made by all Lowe's key executives. The overall goal was to strengthen relationships with suppliers and secure their participation in new marketing efforts.

Top (2): Johnny Walker, Hotpoint hotshot.
Bottom: Carl Buchan at the podium in Charlotte, 1959.

These are excerpts from Carl Buchan's opening remarks:

Gentlemen, this is not going to be a bullshit and sweet potato meeting. We have invited you here to give you the inside story about our firm's operations.

. . .

As you know, we have had many trials and tribulations, but we feel that the most painful period is behind us. We have made many mistakes. Sometimes we have had the wrong people in the wrong jobs, and we appreciate your indulgence during this period of our growth.

. . .

Right now, right this minute, we are at thirty million dollars in sales volume. That doesn't include our tire recapping plant, our oak flooring plant, our three lumber manufacturing plants, or our numerous timber leases. Seven years ago, when I took over complete control and ownership of this business, we had two branches and sales less than two million dollars.

. . .

We are not here to pat ourselves on the back, but to present our future programs and plans. We are having this meeting today because I feel that we are at last ready to do business on a large scale. We have the people— people who not only have the ability to think big, but who have the judgment and business training to properly execute their planning. These boys are red hot: they have the intelligence, the know-how, the experience, and even more important, they have the desire and ambition to play a part in building the world's largest business of its kind.

. . .

What will our future be? If we open just three additional outlets a year for the next seven years (and this is the bare minimum), we will have a total of forty-five outlets, including associate stores, in various parts of these great United States. If each unit does just two million dollars a year, we come up with a total of ninety million dollars worth of business for your company and for mine.

. . .

We want to transmit to you the enthusiasm and the aggressive motivating power of that greatest of all goals— the sale! Gentlemen, my associates and I are happy to swing wide the door of Lowe's Golden Opportunity.

- - -

The Charlotte audience for "Lowe's Golden Opportunity" included more than a hundred vendors.
Carl Buchan on the cover of *Building Supply News*.

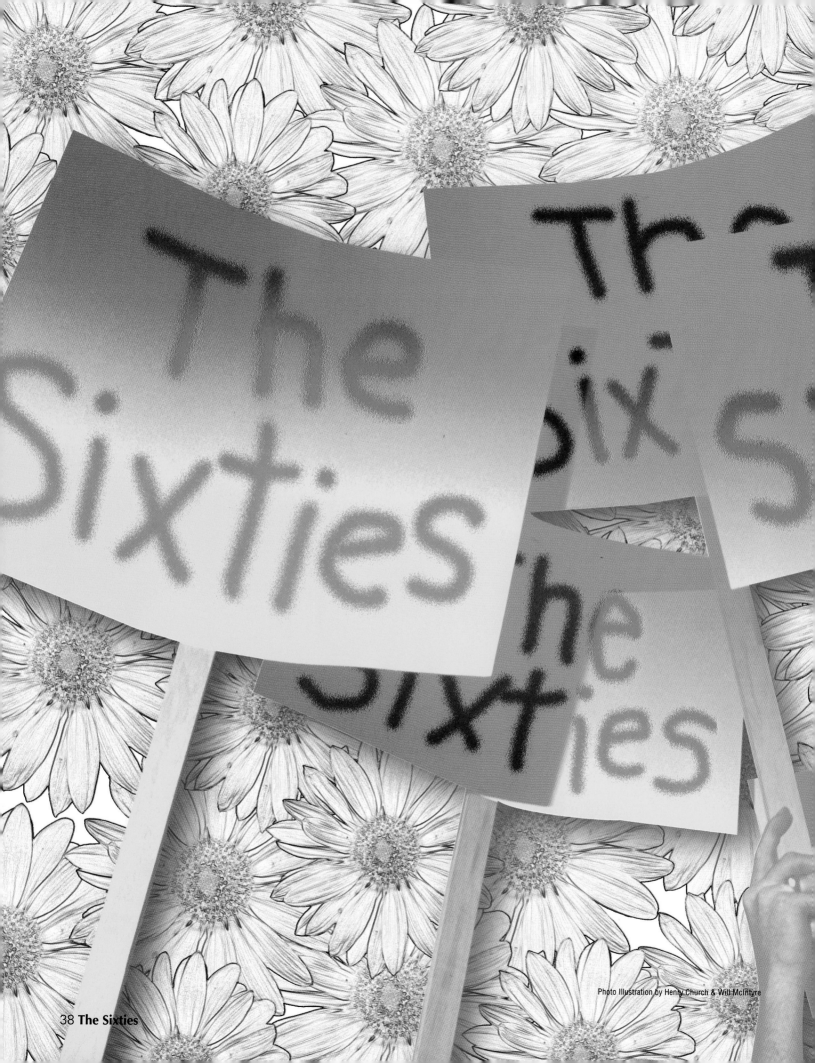

Carl Buchan was 44 years old. He had been president and chief stockholder of Lowe's for eight years. Although it was not yet the coast-to-coast retail giant of his vision, it had come a long way from the little general store that he inventoried in 1943.

Since buying out Jim Lowe in 1952, Buchan had been in the driver's seat— and he had taken his conservative industry on a wild ride. Never before had a retailer attempted to sell directly to consumers, on a "cash-and-carry" basis, everything needed to build a house. Never had one small chain short-circuited the established system of distribution and passed on the savings to its customers.

There were other retailers, such as New York-based Korvettes, who were making a good profit by selling at very small margins, doing high sales volume, and keeping operating costs low. There were other retailers beginning to use computer technology for inventory management. There were other companies who had profit sharing plans, and whose directors at least paid lip service to the desirability of employee ownership. But Carl Buchan was the first to combine all these concepts and strategies under one retail roof.

Was North Wilkesboro, North Carolina an unlikely place for Carl Buchan's retailing genius to bloom? Tell it to Bentonville, Arkansas.

His Army records put his height at five feet, seven inches and his frame as average, although by 1960 it was carrying several pounds more than when he last donned a lieutenant's cap. He gave up drinking and smoking around the time of his split with Jim Lowe; however, Pete Kulynych remembers that "he ate his filet steak for breakfast every morning."

Appropriately for a visionary, he was farsighted: his dark-rimmed glasses magnified his eyes, adding to the impression that he was at best "intense" and sometimes, according to one long-time friend, "staring through you."

He had a memorable voice, often described as a bark, which is still imitated—to chuckles of recognition—among those who knew him.

His circle of intimates was not wide, and he did not casually confide in people. The only hero he ever acknowledged publicly was Robert Hanes of Wachovia Bank ("I worshipped that man," he told an interviewer). During the presidential campaign of 1960, he sent Max Freeman to Beckley, West Virginia with a $5,000 check to help candidate John Kennedy, "because I think he's going to be the next President of the United States." That statement may have been an expression of his personal desire; it was definitely a perception of the marketplace—in this case, for leadership. As always, Carl Buchan's antennae were at full stretch; and, as usual, they were accurate.

America's affluence had grown steadily throughout the Fifties. Every year, more than one million families joined the middle-class (defined as households earning more than $5,000 per year after taxes). By 1960, roughly half of America's forty million families could be counted in that category. *Fortune* called it "an economy of abundance" unprecedented in history.

New houses were going up at the rate of 1.2 million per year. In suburban Charlotte, North Carolina, you could buy a three-bedroom split level house with a bath and a half for $19,250. A two-bedroom rancher with brick veneer and a two-car garage could be yours for $14,950. In 1960, Lowe's supplied materials to build more than 50,000 such houses.

A Lowe's marketing brochure from the early Sixties declared that "We buy right and we sell right. Although manufacturing and distributing costs are increasing, we have been able to reduce the price to the end customer by exercising operational efficiencies, controlling costs, and operating at minimum profit."

With selling margins low, profitability—even minimum profitability—could be achieved only with good cost control. Carl Buchan ran a tight ship, and his insistence on methodical efficiency was generally appreciated by his staff. After all, many of them had

Carl Buchan, circa 1960.

served in the military, and those who hadn't nevertheless understood such concepts as accountability and attention to detail.

The internal financing which was a point of pride with Carl Buchan was made possible in part by a technique that would become obsolete with the advent of electronic data transfer. It was called "playing the float," and Pete Kulynych and Leonard Herring made it an art form.

"Every evening between five and six, all the checks that had been written that day were put on my desk to be signed, along with the latest bank balance," Leonard explains. "I knew which creditors would holler if they weren't paid within a certain amount of time.

"I would estimate the week's cash flow; then I would look at the checks to see how far away they were going. Based on the anticipated cash flow and on the number of days I figured the mail would take, I would decide how many checks I could sign and send out. We lived on the float.

"The only times I lost sleep were when it snowed in our area and deposits stopped coming in, while checks written against those deposits were already in the mail! That's when I sweated."

Carl Buchan knew that the day would come when even the best controls could not guarantee availability of enough capital to finance the growth that he wanted for Lowe's. Edwin Duncan told him "You've got to get more permanent capital in here." So on Duncan's advice, and with the help of accountants Jay Grisette and Ed Beach, Carl Buchan applied for a loan of $1.5 million from the Metropolitan Life Insurance Company.

Leonard remembers, "We didn't have an immediate need for the money; we just wanted to get on their books. Carl said, 'Metropolitan will always have it when we need it.'"

Robert G. Schwartz was a young assistant vice president at Metropolitan when Ed Beach approached him with a proposal for Lowe's. Schwartz proceeded to analyze the company, and almost immediately ran into a snag.

"Because each Lowe's store was incorporated separately, there was no single corporation big enough to guarantee a million-dollar loan," he recalls. "So we put a couple stores together as Lowe's Companies, and the other store corporations served as cross guarantees."

During the process of analysis and preparation known as "due diligence," Bob Schwartz made his first trips to North Wilkesboro. "You had to taxi down a grass runway where they'd cut a swathe out of a cornfield," he says. "Max Freeman would get Lowe's little single-engine plane backed into this cornfield, and he would rev up the engines, the corn would be blowing on either side, and you would take off. It was pretty exciting."

Edwin Duncan, president of Northwestern Bank and longtime friend of Lowe's.

Lowe's Photo Archive

("That's right," Leonard Herring confirms. "And when Max needed to bring in a plane at night, you had to park cars alongside the runway and keep the headlights on so he could see where to land.")

On the first of these trips, Bob met Carl Buchan. "He was a great salesman," Bob recalls. "He convinced me that he could do what he said he'd do. With about fourteen stores, the company wasn't that significant; but the team he had assembled was impressive.

"I asked him why Lowe's was headquartered in North Wilkesboro. He said 'Well, these guys come in every Saturday morning and they work a half day. If we were in Charlotte, do you think I could get them to come in? They'd be out on some golf course.'"

The loan was closed on October 13, 1960 in the legendary board room at Met headquarters in Manhattan. With Carl Buchan were Leonard Herring and Jay Grisette, among others. Bob Schwartz postponed his vacation to make sure the process would go without a hitch. It was one of the first big loans he would make. But at the last minute, Bob himself had doubts.

"At the closing, I hesitated. The stumbling block was Carl Buchan's farm [which he had repurchased from Jim Lowe and stocked with sheep]. When a corporation has a side interest, whether it's a basketball team or a farm, there's a danger that management will divert money and attention from the main business into the side interest. The danger is greater when the company is small, as Lowe's was at the time.

"I almost resolved not to make the loan. Then my counsel took me aside. He was from South Carolina, and he said 'Don't worry about the farm, Bob. All us Southern guys have a little farm, and there's nothing wrong with that.' I said 'Okay, Tom,' and we went back and signed the deal."

Bob Strickland was also in New York, getting ready to go to Bermuda on a trip sponsored by Hotpoint. Carl Buchan telephoned him with the news about the loan.

"He was as happy as I've ever heard him." Bob recalls. "Getting a million was what he'd always wanted. He said, 'I want you to go to Bermuda and have a wonderful time. Come back rested and ready to go to work, because we've got money and we're going to expand this company like you've never seen.'

"It was the last time I talked to him."

On Saturday morning, Carl Buchan's staff assembled for their weekly meeting at the general office downtown. Pete Kulynych, Leonard Herring, Joe Reinhardt, and John Walker were all there, as usual, to review the week's sales results. Bob Strickland was on his way back from Bermuda.

Top: A $1.5 million loan to Lowe's was one of the first big loans that Bob Schwartz made for Metropolitan Life. He would later become Met's chairman.
Bottom: The Met Life Building at One Madison Avenue in New York.

Normally, Buchan would walk through the door on the stroke of nine, fresh from his morning shave at Cyrus McNeil's barber shop. He was never late. But nine o'clock came and went, and he wasn't there.

His staff compared notes; nobody had seen him or heard from him since the previous day. It was unusual—enough so that after just a little while, they decided to call Max Freeman down at the airstrip.

"I answered the phone, and it was Leonard," Max recalls. "He said, 'Have you seen Mr. Buchan? Because he's not here at the meeting, and we thought maybe he'd gone somewhere with you.' I said 'No, we're not supposed to go any-where until tomorrow, but I'll call the farm and see if he's up there.'

"He had been staying up on the mountain, but there wasn't any answer there, so I called Leonard back. Leonard said 'Well, he's got to be around some-where. You'd better go up there; maybe he's overslept.'

"So I jumped in the little single-engine plane, took off right quick, and flew to the farm. Carl Buchan had a Buick station wagon, wood-grained, and it was parked in front of the house. I buzzed the house real low, but nobody came out.

"It was about eleven o'clock by the time I called Leonard again. I said 'His station wagon is at the farm, but he didn't come to the door.' Leonard said 'You'd better drive up there.'"

Max drove over the mountain to the farm, stopping to pick up Bob Farmer, the caretaker. They decided to walk up to the house together.

They rang the bell and beat on the front door, but there was no answer. So Max walked around the outside, looking in windows.

"The curtains in the master bedroom were closed except for one little place where they parted. I looked in and saw Carl Buchan on the bed. It appeared he had come in and sat down on the edge of the bed, then just toppled over. I said to Bob Farmer, 'I believe he's dead.'

"I went around to the back door, jimmied the lock, and went through to the bedroom. He was dead; rigor mortis had already set in. I dialed his doctor up there, and he came right over. He said 'I'll take care of this. Why don't you go find Mr. Duncan? He's prob-ably over at his farm.'

"So there I was. Carl Buchan was dead; it was the end of

October 22, 1960: Leonard Herring and Pete Kulynych took the Presbyterian minister to Carl Buchan's house on Finley Avenue to break the news to Ruth Lowe Buchan.

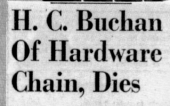

H. C. Buchan Of Hardware Chain, Dies

Heart Attack Fatal at 44

NORTH WILKESBORO—One of North Carolina's biggest success stories ended yesterday with the unexpected death of H. Carl Buchan Jr., 44, who suffered a heart attack at his farm near Sparta at 2 p.m.

A resident of North Wilkesboro, he entered the hardware business in 1945 in partnership with his brother-in-law, Jim Lowe. In 1959 the business, Lowe's Inc., had grossed over $30 million in sales.

Buchan was born Nov. 27, 1915, in Moore County to H. C. and Marie Godfrey Buchan. His pro-

See H. C. Buchan, Page A7

H. CARL BUCHAN JR.
. . . success story . . .

the world. I headed for Mr. Duncan's place, where he was raising sheep, and I met him coming the other way down the road, drinking a Coca-Cola like always. I blew my horn and we stopped traffic. I said 'Mr. Duncan, Carl Buchan is dead. I just left the doctor over at his farm.'

"He told me to go right down and tell Leonard Herring and Pete Kulynych. But when I got back to the office, everyone was gone. So I called Leonard Herring and told him 'Buchan's dead,' and he took it from there."

Says Leonard, "Pete and I went to get Watt Cooper, who was the Presbyterian minister, and we took him to break the news to Ruth Buchan.

"I kept thinking about the night before, when I had seen Carl at the office. It must have been 6:30 or 7:00. I was checking the float, and he was just passing through, but he stopped and talked. He seemed a little fidgety. When he didn't show up on Saturday morning, I knew something had happened."

Bob and Betty Strickland were just getting home when they heard the phone ringing. Bob remembers, "It was Leonard, telling me that Carl Buchan was dead—that his body had been discovered that morning.

"It was shocking; unbelievable. He had been so vital and energetic, and so young."

Carl Buchan had died of a massive heart attack. As word spread, messages of sympathy came from all directions. The Buchan family received telephone calls from Senator John F. Kennedy and his brother, Robert Kennedy. North Carolina's Governor Luther Hodges sent a sympathetic telegram.

The funeral was held two days later; the burial was in Mount Lawn Memorial Park. Pete Kulynych, Leonard Herring, Joe Reinhardt, and Bob Strickland served as pallbearers with Edwin Duncan, Ed Beach, and Bill McElwee, among others.

"Someone at the funeral said 'Well, that's it for Lowe's,'" Bob recalls. "I heard it in the Presbyterian church: 'Lowe's is over.'"

At the Brame Drugstore, a watering hole for leading citizens from old North Wilkesboro families, predictions for Lowe's future were darker than the breakfast coffee. The majority opinion was that Carl Buchan's estate would sell the company to a larger, out-of-town corporation. Others thought that Lowe's stores might be sold individually. Nobody had much faith in the ability of Buchan's young team to hold the company together without him—nobody, that is, except for the team itself.

They were, undeniably, a disparate group with plenty of potential for conflict. The most senior was Pete Kulynych, the self-made man, whose drive to succeed was equalled only by his devo-

This obituary notice ran in *The Winston-Salem Journal.*

tion to his family. Second in seniority, but first in the trust of Lowe's financial and legal associates, was Leonard Herring: a Chapel Hill man from Down East, he was well-grounded and secure, conservative but open to argument. A natural student, he had soaked up the business savvy that he had witnessed at firsthand, first with Henry Weil and then with Carl Buchan.

If Pete had made himself, by constant application, a general factotum for Carl Buchan, then Joe Reinhardt was the opposite: a specialist whose expertise was deep but narrow. As time passed and Lowe's evolved, it was Reinhardt's elastic that wore out first. But in the Sixties, he was a team player who took care of his job and didn't make waves.

Bob Strickland was by nature an intellectual gamesman who would have made his mark on Madison Avenue had he not been captivated by the force of Carl Buchan's personality. Hired for one position and then assigned to another, he adapted. He would find that adaptive skill extremely useful in the coming decades.

John Walker was the impulsive showman, not merely willing but downright eager to take hold of the microphone and step into the spotlight. He once described himself as "an ocean liner, cruising through the water at flank speed, more concerned with maintaining momentum than about what happens to the debris in my wake." When Carl Buchan died, he was the one among the staff who had the biggest salary and the greatest responsibility as defined by his job description. Of the five men, he was the one Carl Buchan had most assiduously courted. Of the five, he would pull hardest in a direction that Carl Buchan never intended for Lowe's.

Lowe's Photo Archive

Lowe's Photo Archive

Lowe's Photo Archive

"I never thought seriously about leaving the company," Bob Strickland says, "and I don't think any of the others did, either.

"It's a tribute to Carl Buchan—because we were bound to him, wanting Lowe's to succeed, wanting to see his vision succeed. He had laid the whole thing out."

Buchan had hired a Washington-based consultant named Burwell to help with his estate planning. The key to everything was an agreement that set the terms under which Lowe's Profit Sharing Plan and Trust could buy Buchan's stock from his estate, so that Lowe's employees would one day own the company.

Top: A hillbilly band plays at Lowe's store in Staunton, Virginia.
Middle: Pete Kulynych, John Walker, and a vendor at Lowe's 1961 "Opportunities Unlimited" program in Charlotte, NC.
Bottom: Bob Strickland at the 1962 opening of Lowe's store in Nashville, TN.

With Burwell's help, Carl Buchan had arrived at a formula for the value of his stock: it was to be sold to the trust at ten times Lowe's earnings for the average of the preceding three years.

"Because I was his finance man, I knew he had been working on it," says Leonard Herring. "One morning in a staff meeting, he told the group what he had planned. We all shook hands with him."

Unfortunately, the agreement was laid out in draft form on Bill McElwee's desk, unsigned, when Carl Buchan died. "We maintained that we had an oral contract with Carl Buchan, even though he didn't live long enough to sign the agreement," Leonard says. This type of oral contract is binding in North Carolina.

The executor of Carl Buchan's estate was Wachovia Bank & Trust. Wachovia hired Bill McElwee to represent the estate in its negotiations with Lowe's. Like politics, estate settlements make strange bedfellows: Bill McElwee had been Lowe's lawyer, as well as Carl Buchan's, but in this situation he decided that working for Wachovia would enable him to apply his understanding in the best interests of all concerned.

"Wachovia hired our lawyer, so we decided to hire theirs," says Leonard Herring. As trustee for the profit sharing plan, he called on Leon Rice at the respected Winston-Salem law firm of Womble, Carlyle, Sandridge and Rice. "I told him about the oral agreement, and how it was backed up by a draft document that hadn't been signed.

"He liked what he heard, and called in Pen Sandridge. Sandridge came in and sat down on the floor and put his knees up, and we all talked. Before I left, the two of them agreed that their firm would represent us."

Lowe's legal team notified the estate that the profit sharing trust intended to exercise its option to buy Carl Buchan's stock. They decided that the company should make a presentation to Wachovia on behalf of the trust. Although John Walker had the highest profile as salesman and showman, Bob Strickland was tapped for the job. "There might have been some concern that Walker would get too angry," Bob muses. "For whatever reason, McElwee asked me to do it. I wish I still had that flip chart. And it may be because I made the

Top: Bill McElwee represented Carl Buchan's executors, Wachovia Bank and Trust Company, in the settlement of his estate.
Bottom: Born in the United Kingdom, Joe Bancroft came to America as a vaudeville performer and later became a pioneer in the aluminum-clad window and door industry. His company, Croft Metals, was a major supplier of doors and windows to Lowe's.

What's In a Name?

In the case of Lowe's logo, quite a lot! Over the years, Lowe's logo has been stretched, squashed, slanted, silhouetted, and adorned with everything from busy beavers to plaid-clad Scotsmen. On this page are just a few of the many corporate signatures that have been used or proposed since 1946.

At right are major steps in the evolution of Lowe's logo.

The top version was common in the Forties and early Fifties, although individual store managers and newspaper ad departments frequently substituted their own variations.

The globe design, which showed up later in the Fifties, was meant to convey expansiveness of vision and scope. Instead, according to Bob Strickland, "it made us look like some kind of travel agency."

In 1965, Strickland made a push for standardization of Lowe's logo into one clean design that could be used on everything from signs to stationery.

A Charlotte designer named Talmadge Moose came close; then Lowe's staff artist Henry Church was assigned to produce a final version (right, middle).

A variation in the 1970's tied the logo to an advertising slogan then in use: "Lowe's, Your Household Word."

The current logo has changed little since 1966. On corporate documents such as the annual report, the name appears with "Companies, Inc." in script.

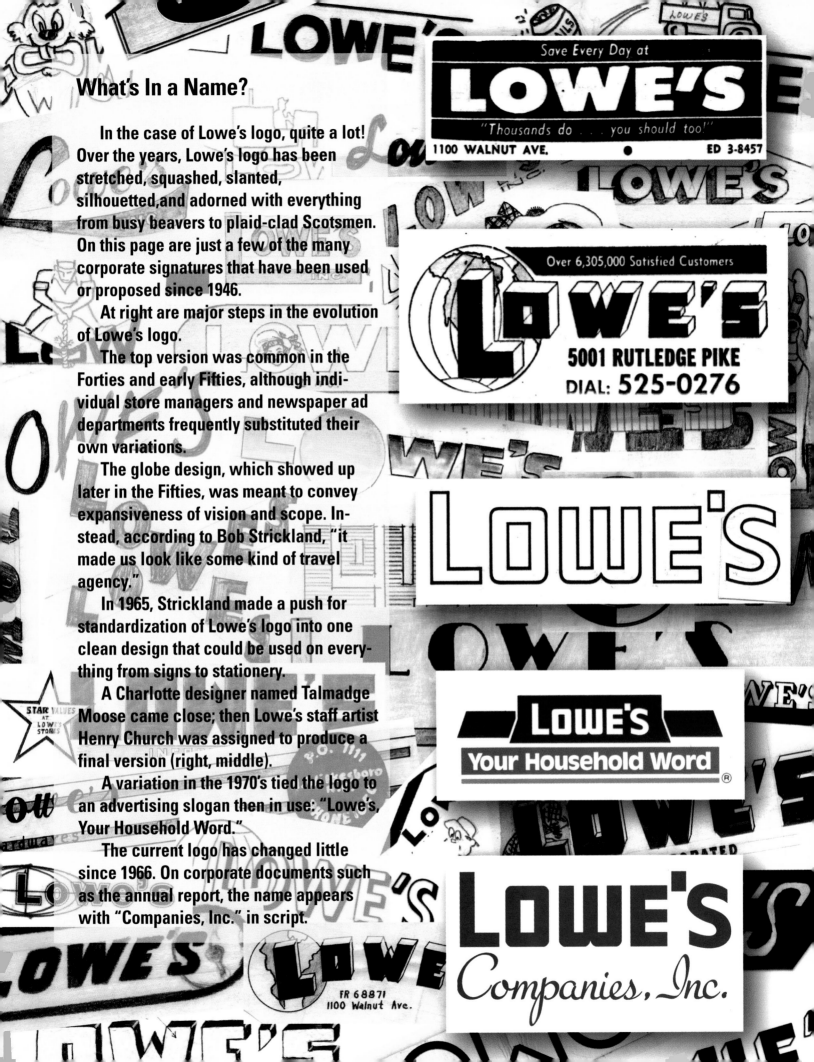

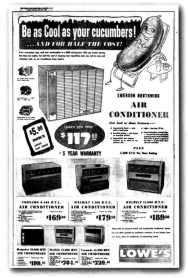

proposal to them that it was Leonard and I who took the lead with the financial people from then on."

Wachovia's trust officers were understandably cautious: their principal obligation was to administer the estate profitably for Carl Buchan's heirs. Carl and Ruth's daughter, Mary Elizabeth, was not yet in her teens. Wachovia didn't want to expose itself to future accusations that it hadn't made the best possible deal for her in the sale of her father's company.

Wachovia decided to consider selling Lowe's to another corporation. "They felt they should put up the company at auction, where they might get more money for it, rather than accept this oral contract that they were told existed," Leonard explains.

Wickes Lumber was known to be interested, but Carl Buchan's team stood together and told Wachovia that they wouldn't work for Wickes. Moreover, if Wachovia tried to sell the company to anyone but the profit sharing trust, they would take their case to court.

Under the cloud of a threatened lawsuit, and without the goodwill of the brain trust that had made it successful, Lowe's appeal for Wickes was substantially diminished. "I don't know if Wickes ever actually made an offer," says Leonard.

Jim Lowe made a brief attempt to get back in the picture. Since his split with Carl Buchan in 1952, his enterprises had included opening a motel, a bowling alley, and a skating rink; starting Lowe's Supermarket (which would become Lowe's Foods); and trying his hand as a racing mechanic with a '57 Oldsmobile driven by stock car ace Junior Johnson. Meanwhile, he had watched Carl Buchan turn the family hardware business into a regional chain worth millions of dollars. Jim Lowe's renewed interest was understandable. But Carl Buchan's team stood together once again to defend his vision for the company, and Jim Lowe remained a bystander.

"After we told Wachovia that we wouldn't work for Wickes, Bill McElwee suggested that the bank consult with Buchan's estate planner," Bob Strickland recalls. "The formula that Burwell and Buchan had devised would set the price for Buchan's stock at roughly $5.3 million. But Wachovia said, 'We know the oral contract would pay $5.3 million, but we've got to have another million on top of that.' In effect, they were asking for almost twenty percent above the price that Buchan had set.

"We argued over that, as you might imagine, but they stuck to it: $6.3 million."

Top: Lowe's annual catalogue included all 3,500 items carried in Lowe's stores.
Middle: In the mid-Sixties, Bob Strickland assumed direct control of Lowe's advertising and launched several new initiatives, including a national print ad campaign.
Bottom: The "cool as a cucumber" newspaper ad was hugely successful and won multiple awards.
Left: Lowe's revolving charge card was a marketing tool introduced in 1965 to help homeowners finance their purchases at Lowe's.

There was about a half million dollars in the profit sharing trust—not nearly enough to leverage $6.3 million. The trust agreed to give the estate a note for $1 million, payable over a period of ten years. But where would Buchan's team get the remaining $5.3 million?

They wouldn't use the loan from Metropolitan Life. Right after Carl Buchan died, Leonard had called Bob Schwartz to assure him that although Lowe's situation had changed, the $1.5 million would be safe. "Bob, I know you've heard the news," Leonard told him, "and we'd be willing to put the loan money in escrow until we get things worked out down here."

"He didn't ask us to do that," Leonard explains, "but it was the fair thing to do, and we wanted a good relationship with Met Life." Indeed, next to the value of the relationship, the $1.5 million loan would one day pale into insignificance.

"We had $500,000 in the profit sharing trust, and we needed more than ten times that much. In effect," says Bob Strickland, "we were trying to do a ten times leveraged buyout, although we didn't call it that in those days.

"Edwin Duncan had good connections with Chemical Bank, and he tried to get them to lend us the money. There was talk back and forth, and Leonard and I flew up with Duncan to see a guy in Chicago; but in the end, nothing worked out."

Leonard recalls other attempts: "A brokerage firm in Charlotte wanted to buy the company and essentially have us work for them. That made us mad.

"The firm of Alex Brown in Baltimore offered to finance the deal in exchange for ten percent ownership. I kept them waiting for an answer as long as I could, hoping that something better would come along.

"Finally, it did. One day, consultant Burwell said 'I know a fellow who would be made to order. His name is Gordon Cadwgan.'"

"Lowe's first came on my scope in April, 1961," Gordon Cadwgan recalls. "Their stores were in the Carolinas almost exclusively. I was based in the Northeast, so I had never heard of them before."

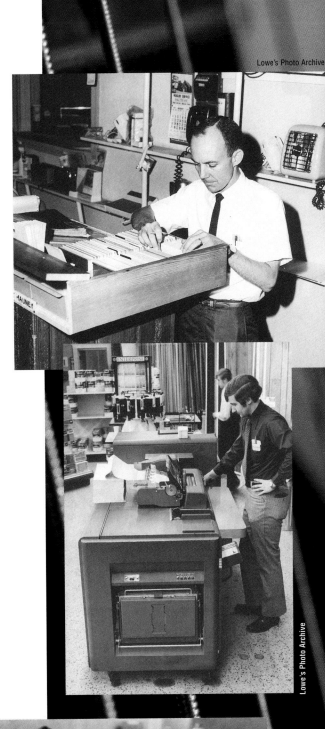

Lowe's was one of the first retailers to use computers for inventory management. The IBM 1401-1311 computer was Lowe's electronic nerve center in North Wilkesboro. Beginning in 1963, compatible sales ticket machines were installed on Lowe's sales floors.

Gordon was working on the west coast of Florida, trying to rescue an investment made by his firm, G.H. Walker & Company of Providence, Rhode Island. One day his home office called to ask if he would talk with a vice president at Wachovia Bank in Winston-Salem about a problematic situation in North Wilkesboro, North Carolina.

"My contact at Wachovia told me about a company whose principal stockholder had died unexpectedly. Wachovia was the executor of the stockholder's estate, and the bank had decided that the best way to get liquidity for the estate was to sell Lowe's Companies to a corporate acquirer.

"Word of this plan had gotten back to the five senior executives who were running Lowe's, and they had descended on Wachovia to say that they strongly opposed the idea of selling the company. It seems they'd had an oral agreement, which had been drafted on paper but not signed, that over twenty years Carl Buchan would sell the company in increments to Lowe's Profit Sharing Trust. But then Carl Buchan had died.

"His estate needed liquidity so that taxes could be paid and the remainder could be invested for the widow and young daughter," Gordon continues. "But if the estate tried to sell Lowe's, these five men would walk. Richard Page was the trust officer for Wachovia. I was sitting in his office in Winston-Salem and I said, 'Well, I don't have an idea in my head at the moment.' Did I want to meet the Lowe's team? 'Yes.'

"In those days, the trip from Winston-Salem to North

Top: The poultry industry has long been a major source of revenue for Wilkes County and the surrounding area. In the early Sixties, John Walker developed and marketed an insulation system for chicken houses which conserved fuel— and fowl!
Middle: John Roselli, a New Yorker transplanted to Wilkes County, opened his popular eatery, Sunny Italy, in a building with chicken house components sold by Lowe's.
Bottom: Lowe's first TV commercial aired in 1968. Los Angeles Rams quarterback Roman Gabriel and stock car superstar Richard Petty were early Lowe's celebrity endorsers.

Lowe's Photo Archive

Wilkesboro was a long, tortuous ride on an old road. I finally arrived in what was then a small, dusty town. I'd been told that the local people didn't like 'revenuers' or Yankees.

"I went to a warehouse-type building, opened the door, walked down a dark hallway, and met the Fab Five for the first time. I think Bill McElwee was there, too.

"I hadn't had any lunch, but they began to tell me their story. Around five o'clock I said, 'Maybe we can find a way.' I told them I'd stay in town overnight, and they all went home.

"I had supper at the little hotel, then decided to go out for a walk. Seeing a big tent on a hill, I headed in that direction and went in. It was a revival meeting! One of the participants asked me if I wanted to be saved; I said 'Not yet.' The next morning, back at Lowe's office, everyone got a kick out of my having wandered unknowingly into a revival.

"These people impressed me. I liked the way they talked—liked their determination not to let go. I told them I could see faint outlines of what might be done, and with considerable help from Strickland and Herring, a plan was devised."

Says Bob Strickland, "Gordon told us he could take Lowe's public for thirteen times earnings. The five of us walked outside Buchan's office, and we all said to each other 'He's the one. He's the one.' We knew it right from the start. He was terrific."

Once the team had decided to take Lowe's public through Gordon Cadwgan, the next step was to borrow money to pay off Carl Buchan's estate. The profit sharing trust had to have ownership before they could proceed with the IPO (initial public offering).

"We were intent on doing this deal the way Carl Buchan

Top: A program featuring entertainer Arthur Smith originated at WSOC-TV in Charlotte and was sponsored by Lowe's.
Bottom: Arthur Smith and his group, circa 1966.

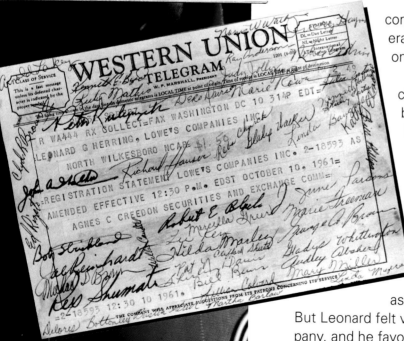

would have wanted," says Bob. But there was another problem: they still lacked some collateral. Then one day, Leonard and Bob were meeting with Gordon at the old Biltmore Hotel in Manhattan, and Leonard suddenly had the idea of pledging Lowe's receivables as collateral.

"Gordon said 'That might do the trick; let me call Herbie Walker!'" says Bob. Herbie Walker was G.H. Walker, principal of Gordon's firm (and uncle of George Herbert Walker Bush). Gordon called him; he called a friend at Guaranty Trust, and the pace accelerated yet again.

Says Leonard, "When I got back home, I was told that in order for the pledging of receivables to be legal, every shareholder had to agree. So we had papers drawn up, and I got in the Cessna 310 with Max, and we flew to every Lowe's location where employees owned stock in individual stores. We would land, they would meet me and sign the papers right there on the wing of the plane, and we'd be off to the next town.

"In a day or so, I had all the signatures we needed."

With the receivables pledged as collateral, Morgan Guaranty made Lowe's a "bridge loan" that paid off Carl Buchan's estate. At that point, Lowe's Profit Sharing Plan and Trust became the owner of Lowe's Companies, Inc., a new entity consolidating all the individually incorporated stores.

Says Leonard, "We had to be just one corporation in order to go public. We considered several names, including Lowe's Enterprises, but decided on Lowe's Companies, Inc."

Edwin Duncan was asked to serve as chairman and president of the new corporation to balance the youth and perceived inexperience of the Lowe's team. He had, after all, been Carl Buchan's financial adviser, and he had a statewide reputation in North Carolina, both for his financial acumen and for his service in the state senate. On top of that, it relieved the Fab Five of the burden of deciding which of them should be elevated to the highest corporate titles.

Not all of them wanted to be relieved of that particular burden. John Walker asked the others, "Why don't we elect one of us?" But Leonard felt very strongly that they should go outside the company, and he favored Edwin Duncan "because he's got the strength for it, and he won't get too involved on a daily basis.

Top: Leonard Herring's copy of the prospectus for Lowe's original public stock offering.
Bottom: A telegram to Leonard Herring from the SEC confirmed Lowe's debut as a public company on October 10, 1961. In celebration, everybody in the general office signed the cable.

"If we stick together," Leonard said, "Nobody can beat us. If we don't, that'll be the end."

The final step was to pay off the bridge loan with funds raised through a public stock offering. Gordon's firm, G.H. Walker, became the lead underwriter. Of one million shares of common stock, Lowe's would sell just enough to repay Morgan Guaranty, with the trading price to be determined on the offering date.

On October 10, 1961, Leonard Herring was in New York. "We set the share price that morning to launch Lowe's as a public company," he says. "Everyone was tremendously excited."

On that first day of trading, roughly four hundred thousand shares were sold at $12.25 per share. That represented forty percent ownership of Lowe's. Another ten percent was owned by the people who had bought shares in Lowe's individual stores.The remaining fifty percent belonged to the profit sharing trust, virtually free and clear.

It was a heady feeling to have this success at last. Carl Buchan's team knew that he would have been proud of their resourcefulness and solidarity through so many challenges. Did they celebrate their triumph?

"No," says Leonard. "We were too tired."

Besides, the next challenge was already waiting.

"Now that we had Lowe's, we had to decide what in the hell we were going to do with it!"

At the beginning of the decade, Lowe's stores typically occupied second-use buildings on three or four acres of land. At 2700 square feet, the average sales floor was not much larger than a

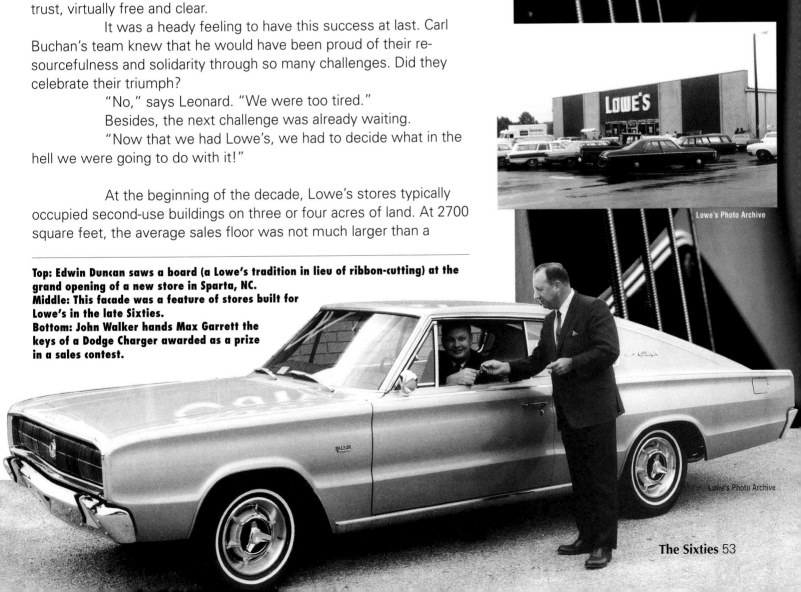

Top: Edwin Duncan saws a board (a Lowe's tradition in lieu of ribbon-cutting) at the grand opening of a new store in Sparta, NC.
Middle: This facade was a feature of stores built for Lowe's in the late Sixties.
Bottom: John Walker hands Max Garrett the keys of a Dodge Charger awarded as a prize in a sales contest.

Lowe's Photo Archive

Lowe's Photo Archive

Lowe's Photo Archive

house. It stocked 1800 items of hardware, building supplies, appliances, and other household goods.

The selection was limited. As Leonard recalls, "If you wanted something to put on your walls, you got wallboard or pine panelling. That was it." The marketing emphasis was on big-ticket appliances, because that's where Lowe's Low Prices really stood out: in building commodity categories, customers were less likely to comparison shop. Although Lowe's had a lumber division which produced flooring and framing lumber, lumber was was not the foundation of Lowe's business.

That changed in the early Sixties, as John Walker urged a redefinition of Lowe's target customer. Carl Buchan had been a mass marketer who saw no reason to focus on a specific customer group. Once, not long after arriving at Lowe's, Bob Strickland was working on a marketing project and wondering aloud about the identity of Lowe's ideal customer.

"I can tell you that," Buchan had said, reaching in his pocket and pulling out his money clip stuffed with cash. "It's anybody and everybody who has any of *this*." But as housing starts climbed, the high volume of professional builder sales was increasingly seductive.

By 1962, the plan for "A Typical Lowe's Store" called for a sales floor of 6,000 square feet, a warehouse of 40,000 square feet, and a storage shed for 150,000 board feet of lumber. Lowe's product offering was being realigned to cater to the professional building contractor, for whom lumber was the staff of life.

That fall, Bob Strickland was elected to a term in the North Carolina House of Representatives and had to delegate most of his marketing responsibilities. Lowe's marketing was divided among three managers by product group: Hal Church took building materials; Emmett Dugger (a friend of Johnny Walker's from Hotpoint) handled appliances; and Mike Brown, who had joined Lowe's in 1957, was in charge of "household goods"—which would now be called consumer products.

From 1963 to 1966, the

Top: Emmett Dugger, marketing manager for appliances and electronics, test drives a tricycle sold as a Christmas promotion.
Bottom: Leonard Herring checks out Lowe's kitchen appliances.
Right: With the shift to contractor sales in the early Sixties, lumber acquired a higher profile.

homebuilder business was booming. Then suddenly it hit the skids. In just six months, the rate of housing starts dropped from 1.6 million to 1.0 million annually. In 1967, Lowe's sales and earnings both experienced their first decline since the company went public. It was time for a strategic adjustment.

New programs were launched in response to the changed business climate. Lowe's product selection was expanded, incentives were offered to remodelers, low-priced utility buildings were packaged and promoted, and marketing once again targeted do-it-yourselfers.

The result was renewed growth in sales and earnings. In 1969, Lowe's joined the ranks of $100 million retailers. It was true that virtually all the growth was the result of adding new stores to the chain: existing stores seemed stuck on $2 million in sales per year. But thanks to good cost controls, profitability was up; and the stock price, which had dipped to $3 in 1962, attained the giddy height of $36 in 1969.

The decade was over; it had been an extraordinary ten years. While Lowe's was coping with the trauma of Carl Buchan's death, dealing with his estate, going public, and reassessing its mission, the country at large had not exactly been basking in the *status quo antes*. Assassinations had taken the lives of John F. Kennedy, Robert Kennedy, and Martin Luther King, Jr. New civil rights legislation had been passed, outlawing discrimination based on race. America had sent troops into combat in Vietnam. Apollo 11 had put men on the moon.

Both Lowe's and America could use a few calm, quiet years to recover. Neither Lowe's nor America would get them.

- - -

Right: Salesman Cat Coleman dresses in pajamas for a Midnight Madness Sale at the Nashville Lowe's store managed by Don Davis.
Bottom: Stagecoach rides were popular attractions at many Lowe's grand openings.

Lowe's Photo Archive

Lowe's Photo Archive

Sixties Hit Parade...1962
Stores: 21   Sales: $32 million   Employees: 491
New stores: Shelby and Hickory, NC; Nashville, TN;
Chattanooga, TN; Huntington, WV; Hagerstown, MD
Popular songs: "Johnny Angel," "I Can't Stop Loving You"

Rome Christie had been selling carpet to Lowe's for years, and had proven his talent for setting up new Lowe's stores—a task that was frequently entrusted to Lowe's major suppliers. In 1962, Rome finally accepted a job offer from Johnny Walker, and was sent to store manager Bob Wessling in Winston-Salem to learn Lowe's (at his own request) from the bottom up.

"On my first day, I reported to the warehouse. Glen Casstevens, the warehouse manager, had never seen me in anything but a white shirt and tie. Now I knew from his smile that I was in for it. He put me to unloading a boxcar of Marquette Cement. Back then, there weren't many forklifts around; I guess we had a pallet jack. So I spent the day unloading those bags one at a time and laying them on a pallet.

"Nobody had to rock me to sleep that night!"

Max Freeman remembers flying Johnny Walker up to Huntington, West Virginia, to check out Lowe's new store just before the grand opening in 1962. "It was next to the river, and the basement was flooded. On top of that, the United Mine Workers were picketing the store. They set up ribbons and lines all around it, and they were standing out there.

"Walker went up to them and said, 'Okay, boys, how much is it gonna cost to join the UMW?' We made peace with them, and they turned out to be good customers. They would come into the store straight from work, and their faces would be so black with coal dust you couldn't recognize them.

"We sold a world of tar paper, and tar, and flat tacks up there, because many people were just building cabins to live in. We made a signboard: 'If you can't flush it, don't use it. Come to Lowe's.' And we would sell a complete toilet system for $99, with everything needed to pump it out to a septic tank. We sold the whole works to them and installed it, too.

"Lowe's was helping get rid of the privies."

In the fall of 1962, Bob Tillman was hired as an office manager trainee by Hal Church, who was managing the Raleigh store. Bob had just moved to Raleigh from his hometown of Mount Olive, and for several months he worked at Lowe's part-time while going to school.

"Then, in the summer of 1963, a deal came up," he recalls. "Lowe's was opening a store in Princeton, West Virginia, and they needed an office manager. There and then, I decided to make my career with Lowe's. I elected to go."

He was nineteen years old.

In October of 1963, Joe Reinhardt hired a young woman named Lucille Johnson, whom he insisted on calling (for reasons known only to him) "Pearl."

"I was hired to code sales tickets," says Lucille. "When I told my Mama that I was going to work for Lowe's, she smiled at me for the first time in I don't know how long."

In those days, every item on every Lowe's sales ticket had to be coded manually so it could be entered in the computer for inventory control. As Lowe's grew, the daily chore got bigger but not more interesting. "We got the job done every day," Lucille says. "But we also got real good at shooting rubber bands.

"On November 22, just a few weeks after I started work, Pete Kulynych came to our room and said 'They've shot the President.' We were all terribly shocked. At the same time, we were almost as shocked that Pete would reveal that he had a radio in the office!"

Joe Reinhardt, Lowe's director of operations, introduced automation to Lowe's sales floors in 1963 with the installation of an IBM 402 computer at the Winston-Salem, NC store.

Stores: 28   Sales: $47 million   Employees: 636

New stores: Vienna, VA; Dover, DE; Wilmington, NC

Popular songs: "A Hard Day's Night," "Can't Buy Me Love"

In 1964, Lowe's locked up the old C Street buildings and moved into new corporate headquarters on Highway 268 East.

That same year, Bill McElwee leased to Lowe's a 40,000-square-foot warehouse which was sometimes called the McElwee Building, but gradually became known by the acronym for Central Office Warehouse: COW.

Already, Lowe's was committed to a centralized system of receiving, consolidation, and storage. This distribution method helped balance inventory among Lowe's stores, and made sense for small town markets as Lowe's merchandise selection expanded.

Before long, such cryptic utterances as "I'm expecting some Mulehide shingles from the COW" were universally accepted and understood throughout Lowe's corporate culture.

Hal Church and Rome Christie were working together in 1964, going from one new Lowe's store to the next, getting them open and then moving on.

"We were up in Dover, Delaware, working like tigers," Rome recalls. "The walls were concrete block, and we'd paint 'em white down to a certain point, then green the rest of the way.

"We were getting ready to open the store the next day, and John Walker came to town. The first thing he did was borrow the company car, a Plymouth straight drive, and he took it downtown and slid into something and dented the fender. He came back raising Cain because I didn't have snow tires on it.

"Then he looked around the store, and he didn't like anything. He wanted it all changed. Well, I'd been driving nails into those concrete blocks, and my fingers were all beat up, and I just looked at Hal, but he said 'Go ahead, take it down.' Just as easy, you know— Hal never did get excited.

"So I got the ladder and started taking stuff down. Pretty soon, Walker decided to go on over to the motel. He got in the car and left, and Hal said 'Put everything back— same holders.' I said 'What?' He said 'Put it back exactly the way it was.' So I did.

"We went down to the motel, had a toddy, ate dinner, and went to bed. The next morning, we went over to the store with Walker. He went in, looked around, and said 'Great job, Rome! That's the way to do it!'

"He was a darn good man, but he had his ways."

1964 was the first year that Lowe's served more than one million customers.

Ross Burgess had joined Lowe's from a struggling associate store in Chester, South Carolina. (Bob Strickland, who ran Lowe's associate store program, says "We didn't get much of a store there, but we got one helluva good man.")

"Lowe's kept that store open a few months," Ross says, "then I moved to Staunton, Virginia, to open a store there. I kept heading north and opened Hagerstown, Maryland, on the very outskirts of Lowe's territory. Then I came back across the Mason-Dixon line and opened Charleston, South Carolina in 1963.

"I remember a sales contest that Johnny Walker ran one Saturday, sometime in the Sixties. The stores were all connected to the general office by teletype. Each store was given a set of sales goals, and you had to report your sales at ten o'clock, noon, two, and four. Whichever store exceeded the goal at ten o'clock would win prize money to be divided among the store personnel. If you won again at noon, it was compounded; and again at two, and again at four.

"You talk about some scrambling! By that four o'clock reading, the stores were in a frenzy.

"Those were wild and woolly years."

Rodney Sterling joined Lowe's in 1965 as the completely fictional creation of Bob Strickland. Rodney was dreamed up by Bob to head Sterling Advertising, Inc., a wholly-owned (and very real) Lowe's subsidiary.

Sterling Advertising was created from Lowe's internal advertising department because media outlets such as radio stations gave independent ad agencies discounts and commissions that they didn't extend directly to corporate advertisers.

Henry Church had been working on Lowe's advertising with Jack Patterson in Charlotte, but he moved back to his hometown of North Wilkesboro at Bob's invitation.

"I thought a fictional boss would be easy to work for," says Henry. "Boy, was I wrong!"

No sooner had he settled into Sterling's leased offices than Henry's phone started ringing off the wall.

"Bob had sent out bunches of letters to introduce the agency and request rate information, all under the name of Rodney Sterling," Henry explains. "I had to make excuses for Rodney and try to get people to talk to me instead. Some of them demanded to know 'When will Mr. Sterling be in?'"

If you read this, Rodney Sterling, please call your office.

The switched-on sound of the '60's is that of an amplified electric guitar. In 1966, Lowe's added a complete line of acoustic and electric guitars, and amplifiers.

In its first year at Lowe's, the guitar line became the third largest category of home entertainment merchandise, surpassed only by televisions and radios.

— Lowe's 1966 annual report

1966
Stores: 39 *Sales: $77 million* *Employees: 891*
New stores: Woodbridge, Newport News,
and Suffolk, VA; New Castle, PA
Popular songs: "Cherish," "The Sounds of Silence," "Wild Thing"

Lowe's first Hootenanny was convened at the Elks Club in North Wilkesboro in 1963. Its purpose was to introduce new products, principally for the Christmas selling season.

"Transistor radios might have been introduced at that first hootenanny," says Bob Strickland.

"It was perhaps a couple years later, and John Walker was doing his thing at a hootenanny, showing people how to sell appliances. He would take a quarter and bang it down on a range top to show that the baked porcelain couldn't be scratched. Or he'd pour some lighter fluid on it and set fire to it.

"Back in those days, GE had a safety screen on their console TV's so you couldn't touch the picture tube. John had been trained in making presentations to his sales force, and he'd say 'They're tough, don't worry about anything,' and he would hit them with his fist— whap whap whap!

"Well, we had a line of TV's on the stage, and John didn't know that these things didn't have a safety glass. He said 'I just want to show you how tough these things are—,' and he whapped on a 21" screen, and the whole picture tube fell right out of the case!"

1967
Stores: 44   Sales: $76 million   Employees: 1017
New stores: Charlotte (2nd) and Whiteville, NC; Greenville, SC;
Charlottesville, VA; Charleston, WV; and Salisbury, MD
Popular songs: "Respect," "Ode to Billie Joe," "Light My Fire"

In February of 1967, David Sain shipped out to Dong Tam Kan Thau, South Vietnam, for a one-year tour of duty in the army. He and his wife, Evelyn, were newlyweds.

He was born in 1946, the year of Lowe's rebirth in the postwar era. Maybe that's why, according to his mother, David's very first word was "Lowe's!"

He grew up and finished high school in Hickory, NC, and was a community college student when he was drafted into the army on Valentine's Day in 1966.

He came home from Vietnam in February of 1968, interviewed with John Walker the following month, and was hired as a sales trainee assigned to his hometown store, which was managed by Pete Miner.

Several years later, David would manage that same Hickory store through an expansion which doubled its size but caused roofing problems and leaks. One day, while he was reviewing his financial statement during a hard rain, the entire suspended ceiling fell on him, and David's head went through a ceiling panel.

The hazards of Vietnam were basic training for life at Lowe's!

1968   Sales: $97 million   Employees:1,223
Stores: 53
New stores: Lumberton, NC; Anderson, Columbia,
Myrtle Beach, Manning, and Sumter, SC; Frankfort, KY;
Hopewell, VA; Blytheville, AR
Popular songs: "Mrs. Robinson," "Sittin' on the Dock of the Bay"

By the end of the decade, Lowe's success as a public company was receiving plenty of attention in print. Lowe's was included in "101 Growth Stocks" and "A New Look At Growth," published by Merrill Lynch; "33 Super Growth Stocks," published by Standard and Poor's, and "Baby Blue Chips" in *Forbes.*

"A tiny cartridge called a 'cassette,'" said Lowe's annual report in 1968, "is making rapid headway as the all-purpose tape recording system. It may eventually replace LP albums."

The 1968 annual report praised manufacturers of cooking ranges for an innovative new feature: the self-cleaning oven.

Although Larry Stone grew up in North Wilkesboro, he reached the age of seventeen without really knowing much about Lowe's. He had never heard of Leonard Herring until his job interview, but he was grateful when Leonard hired him to work part-time in Lowe's mail room and print shop.

He started with Lowe's on June 2, 1969 for the hourly wage of $1.60, and he still has the stub from his first paycheck—for $67.36.

The denizens of the mail room were not unanimously thrilled with their earning power at Lowe's. "Some of them said 'You can't make any money here,'" Larry recalls.

"But two months after I started, Mr. Herring came back to the mail room. Right in front of everybody, he said to me 'I like the way you've been running this department.' Then he gave me a ten cent raise.

"Man, I was tickled to death. I was up to $1.70. That was big money."

In the late Sixties, purchasing manager Bob Black went with Rome Christie to call on Armstrong Flooring in Lancaster, Pennsylvania.

"Armstrong was still very distributor-oriented at that time: they wouldn't sell to anybody else," Rome says.

"We went in, and there were all these guys in black suits sitting behind desks, each in his own office. They sent us from one to the other, and none of them could make a decision.

"That evening, we went to the president's house for dinner. I told him that if Armstrong was ever going to do business with Lowe's, they were going to have to put one man in charge of it. We didn't have time to talk to all those people, then wait for them to get together and make a decision; Armstrong needed somebody who could coordinate all that and have an answer ready for us when we came to town.

"And you know what? Armstrong took our advice!"

Lowe's had come a long way.

Illustration by Henry Church

GIMME SHELTER!

1970: The Beatles split up and the first Boeing 747 took off. The price of oil surged; the price of everything else followed. American troops invaded Cambodia, igniting a firestorm of controversy at home. Four students were killed by national guardsmen during an antiwar protest at Kent State University in Ohio.

The U.S. Senate passed a bill prohibiting cigarette advertising on radio and TV. The Environmental Protection Agency was established, and the first international Earth Day was celebrated. At a free Rolling Stones concert at Altamont in California, a fan was killed by Hell's Angels who had been hired (no joke) to provide security. The heavyweight boxer formerly known as Cassius Clay returned to the ring as Muhammad Ali and won his first two fights.

In Atlanta, Georgia, a struggling UHF television station was bought by a businessman and sports enthusiast named Ted Turner, who renamed it WTBS and began broadcasting its low-cost programs by satellite to cable systems around the country.

Like the senior Baby Boomers in the counter-culture, Lowe's was twenty-four years old in 1970. If it had been a young adult, Lowe's might have burned its bra, smoked a little pot, and cranked up the Grateful Dead. But at Lowe's the only counter-culture that mattered was the one gathered around its sales counters— and things were wild enough there to make the rest of the world seem tame!

Dwight Pardue had been manager of Lowe's store #13 in Richmond, Virginia since Carl Buchan sent him to open it in 1959.

"Broad Street was (and is) a great location," Dwight says. "We did good retail business there, as well as contractor sales. We were the first Lowe's store to stay open until nine at night.

"We were the first Lowe's store to stock lumber. We were doing so much contractor business, we sold a carload of mortar every day. We'd have a rail car on the track and two more waiting, all the time.

"The leading homebuilder in Richmond had two brothers who were also builders. I was determined to get his account, so I assigned one of our delivery trucks exclusively to him. We gave him such good service that he got me on the board of the homebuilders association.

"Our local competition was Republic Lumber Company and the Moore's chain. In fact, Richmond was Moore's headquarters.

"Moore's was in a different part of town, but we took so much of their business that they opened another store on the street behind us. Know what we did? We routed all our delivery trucks past their store, so they could see how much business we were doing. It drove them crazy.

"John Walker had been personally managing every store in Lowe's chain. He wanted to do everything himself: he was on the road all the time. He used to come up to Richmond once a month, and we would lay out a month's advertising in his hotel room.

"Finally, the rest of the Executive Committee talked Walker into giving up management of the stores. They made him use Al Plemmons and me as regional vice presidents. We were appointed on August 1, 1970. One month later, Walker had a heart attack.

"He was out for six or eight weeks, and we had no guidelines. We had to figure out our own schedules and set up everything. We invented our own supervisory system.

"Lowe's was buying and opening stores at a frantic pace. If we wanted experienced people, we had to train them ourselves and move them around. Stores had their own credit offices and carried their own receivables. We got a lot of guidance from [Lowe's credit manager] Arnold Lakey.

Dwight Pardue was one of Lowe's first regional vice presidents.
All uncredited photos are from Lowe's Photo Archive.

"I would leave North Wilkesboro on Monday morning, hit a store and check the receivables, the warehouse, and the office procedures. That night we would have a sales meeting for sales personnel and an office meeting for office personnel. Then it was on to the next store.

"We tried to visit each store every three or four weeks."

A native of Shelby, North Carolina, Frank Beam had been managing his hometown Lowe's for three years when the Seventies began.

"We were doing contractor business, and most of the competition was local," he says. "They were family stores that were inherited—that type of thing. Most of our competitors were connected to savings and loan boards, so when building permits were issued, we were competing with those community contacts. It was very clannish. That's why we used to have to 'buy the business' at first, by cutting our prices. You had to get the builders into the store before you could develop a relationship."

Don Davis had a knack for getting people's attention. As newly appointed manager of the Nashville store in the mid-Sixties, he had a problem: "There was a Purina feed mill at the end of our street, but no other retailers nearby. People just didn't pass by our store.

"We had to bring 'em out there, and do it with the limited funds in our advertising budget. We had to use everything available to us."

He conceived the idea for a Midnight Madness Sale which began at 12:01 a.m. and ended with salesmen in pajamas serving breakfast to their early-bird contractor customers.

"A lot of new people came out and saw how friendly we were, and what good prices we had. We took a lot of business away from our competitors."

Then there was the time Davis decided to "declare war on high prices."

"There was a national guard armory not far from the store. I had never met the commander, but I went to see him and said 'I want to borrow a tank.'

Top: The contractor sales "bullpen" was where sales were made and paperwork was generated.
Bottom: Ross Burgess (right) and Hayden Johnson in a Lowe's lumber yard.

"I'll never forget the look on his face. He said, 'You want *what?*' So I told him Lowe's was declaring war on high prices, and he said 'That's fantastic.'

"I told him I wanted to shoot the tank. He said 'You can't shoot it: it would blow the windows out of your building.' I said 'I don't want it to have a shell in it; I just want it to make noise and shake the ground.'

"He told me the noise would still knock the windows out of cars in the parking lot. Then he said, 'I've got some jeeps and some half tracks; you can use them if you want.' So that's what we did, and we had airplanes and skydivers too. We had people lined up around the block. It was like a fair out there."

Although he weighed about 300 pounds at the time, Don dressed up as Uncle Sam. "I came through the front door of the store just a-truckin'. A little boy looked up at his mother and said 'Mama, look at that big fat Uncle Sam!' And the woman said 'Son, that's what inflation has done to him.'"

Johnny Walker hired Ben Phillips in 1969 to build a mobile home business within Lowe's. Mobile homes had improved immensely since the postwar housing shortage, both in appearance and engineering, and financing was always available for mobile homes because it paid higher interest to the investor than mortgages on traditional houses. As a result, the late Sixties had seen a tremendous increase in mobile home sales. Walker, who often identified himself as Lowe's "vice president of sales *and profits*," sniffed an opportunity in the wind.

"I told him there was a mobile home trade association in Chicago, and I thought I should go up there and learn what I could," Ben recalls. "I was on the plane the next morning. That began an adventure that ended with Lowe's having twenty or thirty sales centers for mobile homes that we called Ranchettes.

"Then we got the Homestead business cranked up. The

Top and bottom: The Ranchette was Lowe's entry in the mobile home business. They sold for about $7,000 (furniture, phone, and family members not included).

idea was conceived one day on an airplane coming back from looking at a manufactured housing business in Virginia. Someone said 'They assemble a home in a factory. Why can't we put together the basic materials for a home at Lowe's?' That's how the Homestead program grew out of the Ranchette business."

Lowe's Homestead was introduced in 1971. Designed by an architect, it was a small house of about 1,000 square feet. All its component materials from foundation to roof were grouped for delivery in a normal building sequence. Importantly for Lowe's sales force, each item on the materials list had a code number and a quantity indicated. That way, a salesman could run prices on the entire house package at any time, and the total would reflect the latest pricing changes. The purpose was to offer Lowe's customers a better home at a lower price than modular housing, with many of the advantages of on-site construction.

The first Homestead packages, which included everything except labor and land, sold for less than $4,500. In a way, it was the culmination of Carl Buchan's philosophy.

"It was the first major attempt at one-stop shopping for homebuilders," says Ben Phillips. "For one price, you got everything you needed to build a house. The Homestead program was like a marketing umbrella, because it made the big statement that Lowe's had it all."

As Ben remembers it, life at Lowe's in the early Seventies was "like being on a mission. We knew no barriers.

"We had two speeds: 'stop,' and 'wide open.' It wasn't unusual to leave on Monday, come back on Saturday, and leave again the following Monday. We were opening stores left and right.

"We were caught up in an incredible dream. It was energized: you can see that in old Hootenanny pictures. We worked hard and we played hard. Quite frankly, life at Lowe's was a combination

The first Homestead houses were very simple, but the line expanded to include more elaborate models as the concept proved successful.

of work and play—and you had to be careful not to get them out of balance."

There was more than one balancing act under Lowe's big top. In Carl Buchan's time, management functions and responsibilities had been fluid, not formal: the company was small, and the staff did whatever needed to be done. After his death, however, the ambiguities and inequities in the management structure became collecting points for confusion. The company had grown larger and more complex, and each of the Fab Five now had days when the burden of responsibility seemed greater than its rewards.

Edwin Duncan had been chosen by the team to be chairman and president because of his familiarity with the company and his credibility in the financial community. As Leonard had predicted, he was basically a hands-off executive who let the team run Lowe's as they knew best.

"He lived at his farm and drove down every day to his office at Northwestern Bank," Leonard says. "He would drop by Lowe's occasionally, to see how things were going and what was making a profit."

He was a big man with an odd habit of chewing on his silk neckties. He had a keen eye for sizing up character, but didn't volunteer his opinions freely. "If you wanted to know something, you had to ask him," Bob Strickland says.

Leonard appreciated the chance to learn from yet another mentor. "Edwin Duncan trained me," he says. "When Carl Buchan died, I was 32 years old. I got more financial education in a couple of years than most people get in a lifetime."

Duncan's other function, tacitly accepted by the team, was "to sit on us and hold down the intramural squabbling, when necessary," says Bob Strickland. "Of course, he was smart enough to know that a certain amount of that was healthy."

Pete Kulynych recalls that for a while, at least, consensus was the norm in executive committee meetings. "I think we only had a few real 'votes,'" he says. "There were five of us, so theoretically you could win if you had three votes, but we hardly ever did it that way. It was usually a consensus.

Edwin Duncan gave guidance and support to Lowe's management team.

"If you strongly disagreed with what someone else was presenting, you would stand up and say 'I've gotta go to the bathroom.' And that killed it.

"Of course, everyone has an ego. Some you could put in a teacup; others won't fit indoors." When egos clashed, it was Duncan who sorted things out. "He was the sounding board," says Pete. "His job was to put our heads together—knock 'em together if necessary—and see that we came out friends."

In his 1970 letter to shareholders, Duncan said "During this year it became obvious to me that an important stage in the growth and development of Lowe's had been reached, and that it was time to reorganize our management structure." He created a committee to study the problem and make a recommendation. He appointed Pete Kulynych and John Walker to the committee, and made Bob Strickland the chairman.

Since the day Carl Buchan hired him, John Walker had been paid more than anyone else on the team. "John honestly thought the difference was justified," says Bob, "and I think he continually tried to justify the difference." Nevertheless, the disparity was a source of conflict.

Aggravating other differences of opinion, concerns about pecking order threw off the gear ratio among the five wheels of the executive committee. For a while, the only ill effect was an occasional grinding noise; now, however, it was slowing down the whole works.

Bob Strickland's *ad hoc* committee recommended that the gearbox be rebuilt. Of the five-man team and Edwin Duncan, the one least likely to press his claim to Lowe's presidency was the man who actually held the title.

The committee recommended that the presidency be shared among the five members of Carl Buchan's hand-picked team, and that it be known as the Office of the President. Edwin Duncan would stay on as board chairman The idea was unconventional, but Lowe's had a history of successfully defying conventional wisdom.

Says Bob, "Duncan had wanted us to tell him what could and should be done. Now I had to go to him and ask him to relinquish the title of president—and take a cut in salary!"

Top: The COW, Lowe's first Central Office Warehouse.
Bottom: Richard Spivey, Lowe's resident computer wizard. Some thought he was weird, but in fact he was wired. He programmed and de-bugged Lowe's IBM machines, and was on call 24 hours a day.

Duncan agreed: he thought the new structure might work. So did Bill McElwee, who was then a vice president as well as Lowe's general counsel and a member of the board.

The Office of the President was established with Pete and John as executive vice presidents, and Leonard, Bob, and Joe as senior vice presidents. Bill McElwee was also elevated to the status of senior vice president. At the same time, Dwight Pardue and Al Plemmons were confirmed as Lowe's first regional vice presidents.

Ben Phillips considers the Office of the President to have been the perfect management structure for Lowe's at that time.

"We got the best of five peers," he explains. "The beautiful part was that each one had a distinct personality. They weren't clones of each other.

"We had Pete, a logistics genius. We had Bob directing marketing from the top of the pyramid. We had Leonard, who could turn a dime into eleven pennies. We had Reinhardt, who understood warehousing, construction, and the distribution side. And we had John, who was bouncing off every wall with more energy than a locomotive and more charisma than most people will be exposed to in their entire lives.

"What a combination of talents! The team Carl Buchan put together was the envy of the industry."

In 1971, Lowe's was one of 2,500 stocks selected by the National Association of Securities Dealers to be quoted on the new NASDAQ, a computerized quotation network. That year, according to an independent review, Lowe's ranked fiftieth in market value among the more than 26,000 over-the-counter stocks in the nation.

Lowe's was a darling of Wall Street. Principal among its charms was the fact that since going public in 1961, Lowe's earnings per share and shareholders' equity had both been growing at an average rate of twenty percent each year. Leonard, Bob, and John had success-

The Office of the President: (L. to R.) Kulynych, Strickland, Herring, Reinhardt, and Walker.

fully divided the investor relations obligations of a public company. As Bob puts it, "John did the talking, I did the writing, and Leonard did everything else."

"My job as finance officer changed a lot when we went public," Leonard explains. "We had to start reporting to the Securities and Exchange Commission, and there were lots of additional accounting procedures and other new responsibilities."

Leonard's skillful financial management won high praise from the analysts who studied retail stocks. When it came to marketing Lowe's as an investment, however, Leonard was happy for John Walker to handle the courtship rituals of Wall Street.

"John became known as the point man for Lowe's investor relations because he was making all the presentations to Wall Street," says Bob. "He was wonderful at it—a real *artiste*. There was never any conflict between us over who did what: I knew I couldn't talk, and he knew he couldn't write!"

Bob assumed responsibility for presenting Lowe's to the investment community in print. For the first few years, Lowe's annual reports were stylistically conservative and brief, with no attempt to be comprehensive in scope.

"Our 1964 annual report actually said 'Space does not permit a full account of our winning combination,'" Bob recalls. "And with just twelve pages, it really didn't!" However, as Lowe's grew in size and confidence as a public company, the annual reports became livelier and more discursive.

In 1968, Bob decided to feature a description of Lowe's organization in all its aspects. The annual report won a Bronze Oscar in *Financial World* magazine's juried competition recognizing the year's outstanding financial statements. In 1969, Bob added contextual economic and demographic information, and that report was awarded a Silver Oscar.

Courtesy of Matt Phelan

Top: Early Lowe's stock certificates. Lowe's stock was one of the first 2,500 to be quoted on the NASDAQ.
Bottom: Arnold Lakey, Lowe's vice president and credit manager, circa 1975.

The 1971 report celebrated Lowe's tenth anniversary as a public company. It reviewed the company's growth, discussed trends in consumer spending, financing, and merchandising, and concluded with a corporate history. It won the coveted Gold Oscar from *Financial World*, edging out strong competition from the likes of Continental Air Lines, General Electric, Philip Morris, and Xerox.

The October 25, 1972 issue of *Financial World* featured Bob Strickland on the cover and a discussion of Lowe's annual report inside:

Full financial data, product lines, sales analyses, relevant industry and customer statistics, performance of the company compared with its competitors—these are some of the ingredients that are presented so comprehensively and clearly as to cause a judge to comment that "no other annual comes within hailing distance of the Lowe's report."

It was another validation, another proof that a company which started as a small-town hardware store in the Southern mountains could hold its own in the big leagues of corporate America.

Dick Griffin's first memory of John Walker goes back to a Chicago trade show in 1972, when Dick was working for Sears.

"John was the keynote speaker," Dick says. "He came into the hall flanked by security guards who accompanied him to the podium. There he brought out a million dollars in cash, and set it on top of his keynote address. He said 'If you stick with Lowe's, you can make a million dollars.'

"I don't know if it was really a million dollars or not, but it blew everybody's mind. He probably had a thousand dollar bill on top, another on the bottom, and paper in the middle, but everyone believed he had a million."

Bob Tillman was managing Lowe's store in Wilmington, North Carolina. On his watch, it would be a test site for virtually every

Top: When Lowe's 1971 annual report won the prestigious Gold Oscar from *Financial World*, the magazine featured Bob Strickland on its cover.
Bottom: Previously a retail analyst with the National Shawmut Bank in Boston, Deborah Kelly became Lowe's first vice president for investor relations.

new phase in Lowe's evolution. Hal Church had persuaded him to leave the safety of the office in 1965 and get out on the sales floor, where the guaranteed salary was minuscule but a good salesman could do well on commission. Bob served as assistant store manager for a while under Bill Cothren, and became store manager when Cothren retired in 1969.

In 1968, the decision was made to divide Lowe's sales force into builder and retail segments with specialized training for each. "At about the time I became store manager, Wilmington became the first store to take contractor salesmen off the sales floor," Tillman says. "We gave them an office in the warehouse near the loading dock, and in that way we physically separated our two businesses."

Sales to professional contractors accounted for roughly seventy percent of Lowe's total business in 1968. Throughout the Seventies, despite the swoops and surges of housing starts, building contractors would remain Lowe's dominant customer group.

Marketing to contractors gave the corporate culture a distinctly macho flavor. For more than 25 years, one of Lowe's most popular incentive programs awarded points on contractor purchases toward an annual free trip to Las Vegas. They were mostly stag trips: wives were accepted, but children were absolutely prohibited.

"At first we stayed at the Frontier or The Dunes," Bob Tillman recalls. "Then Caesar's Palace was built, and we started going there.

"Las Vegas was honky-tonk back then—there was a lot of gambling, drinking, and chasing. It had nothing to do with children, except that a lot of children were probably conceived there!"

Wild as it was, these were working trips. "We had business meetings with all these people," Dwight Pardue explains. "Ben Phillips and I would go out there and stay for ten days or two weeks at a time.

Bob Tillman first made his mark on the company as a store manager in Wilmington, NC. He was so involved in civic organizations that he became known as "Mr. Wilmington."

Arnold Lakey would come, too: as Lowe's credit manager, he wanted to have faces to put with the names on big builder accounts.

"Every four days a new group of customers would come in, and we would put on a show. There was always a new merchandising program to announce: one year it was the Homestead package; another time it was a truss program. There was always something to help us generate additional business. Manufacturers would come with displays that would be open in the afternoon and evening."

"It was hard work," says Dick Griffin, who came to Lowe's from Sears in 1976. "We would take a group out there and wine and dine them for four days. When we were about ready to drop, the next group would come in. They didn't know about the first group, and they didn't give a damn."

Bruce Ballard had joined Lowe's at the Asheville store in 1962. In the Seventies, he was managing the Raleigh store and taking groups of forty or fifty builders to Las Vegas every year.

"Those were special times, and the relationships we built were special, too," Bruce says. "There were builders like Jud Ammons, who started out as a customer but became one of my closest friends. Steve Myrick, too—he's a great guy who started as a great customer."

Some builder trips went to even more exotic places, such as London, Montreux, and Maui.

"We would take three or four hundred of Lowe's very best customers," Bruce says. "There was lots of interaction. It wasn't like we took them over there and turned them loose and said 'Go have a good time.' We created loyalty through the experiences that we shared, and we have customers who still remember those things."

In 1972, John Walker ran for lieutenant governor of North Carolina on the Republican ticket.

Top: Dwight Pardue forgoes formality to address a gathering of Lowe's best contractor customers at Caesar's Palace in Las Vegas.
Middle: On a trip to San Juan, Puerto Rico, salesmen and store managers searched for buried treasure on the beach. Johnny Walker, left, applauds Bill Cockerham's discovery of the loot.
Bottom: The winner of a new car in a sales contest celebrates with a cigar. So much for that "new car" smell!

His opponent was a lawyer from "down East" named Jim Hunt.

Walker was not the first Lowe's executive to run for office. Bob Strickland had served in the state House of Representatives; before him, Edwin Duncan had served several terms in the North Carolina Senate. But Walker was the first to mount a statewide campaign and to spend more than $600,000 of his own money on the effort.

Although he had been politically active behind the scenes since switching parties several years earlier, he was still unknown to the typical Tarheel voter. The Republican gubernatorial candidate, Jim Holshouser, kept him at arm's length. Not for the first time, Johnny's critics shook their heads at the patented Walker combination of *chutzpah*, charm, and naiveté. His supporters, while hoping for the best, secretly believed that this time Johnny had bitten off more than he could chew.

Knowing himself to be a consummate salesman, Johnny declined the assistance of professional media consultants in his campaign. At the same time, he relied heavily on broadcast media to replace one-on-one contact with the public. He declared that he would walk across the state in the course of his campaign, but gave up the idea "after getting hit by a beer can and a tomato, and bitten by a dog," as he explained to one reporter. With no grassroots organization, and with television commercials that were more entertaining than persuasive, Walker had no chance against the man who would become one of the most successful and popular governors in North Carolina history. He lost by a margin of 57 to 43 percent. But as always, he had enjoyed the game.

Jim Hunt smiles when he remembers that campaign. "It was my first statewide race, and it was all the more interesting because Johnny Walker had so much enthusiasm and energy," says the governor. "Those are the same qualities that had made him a great salesman for Lowe's.

"He had a caring spirit, and in years to come we found ourselves agreeing on a number of things."

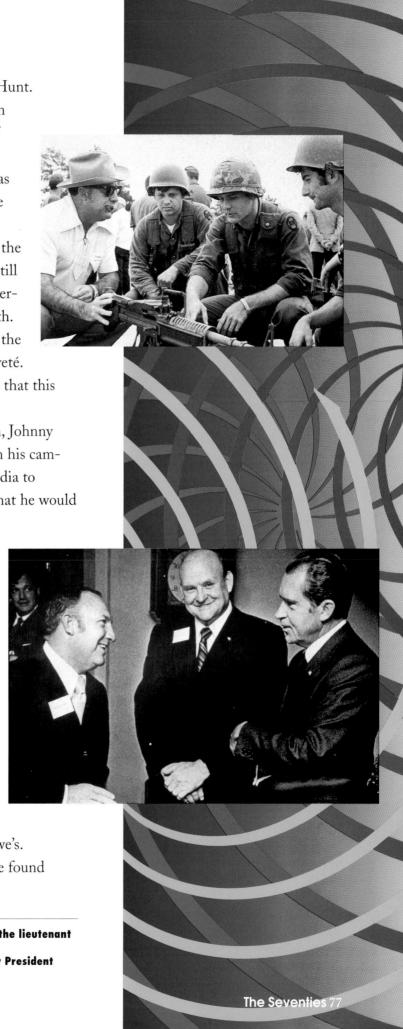

Top: Johnny Walker with national guardsmen during his 1972 run for the lieutenant governorship of North Carolina.
Bottom: As a Republican candidate for office, Walker was welcomed by President Richard Nixon at the White House.

Four years later, Walker decided to endorse Jim Hunt for governor over the Republican candidate, I. Beverly Lake. A newspaper reporter confronted Johnny and asked "Why are you endorsing your former opponent, the man who defeated you, over the candidate of your party?"

"Well," said Johnny, "I think Beverly Lake is too much of a radical conservative."

"A radical conservative!" the reporter repeated. "Then what do you call Jesse Helms?"

"I call him 'Senator Helms,'" Johnny replied, smiling serenely. "What do *you* call him?"

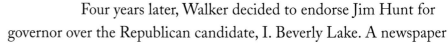

In 1973, Edwin Duncan died of natural causes. He had been chairman of Lowe's board of directors since the company went public twelve years earlier. The board decided not even to try to replace him as chairman; instead, Pete Kulynych agreed to serve as acting chairman, and Bob Schwartz, who was now a vice president at Met Life, was nominated as a new outside director.

Lowe's directors published a memorial tribute that included the following insights to the character of Ed Duncan:

He was a fascinating and complex person who treated his phenomenal successes and remarkable capabilities with a casualness born of genuine modesty and humility. He was essentially a private person who enjoyed the solitude and beauty of his small mountain town, the warm closeness of his family, and the company of old friends. He was equally at home with the security analyst, the corporate executive, the educator, the politician, and the farmer.

Lowe's had lost its father figure.

Top: Lowe's original Audit Committee: Gordon Cadwgan, Bill McElwee, Bob Schwartz, and Jay Grisette.
Bottom: Hal Church was one of Lowe's first millionaire retirees. When he retired, his friends at Lowe's gave him a golf cart to propel him through his new leisure hours.

By the fall of 1974, it was no news to most Americans that the economy was in trouble. In the wake of the Arab-Israeli War, oil-producing Arab countries had cut back oil production and put an embargo on oil shipments to the United States. The price of energy had gone up like a gas jet, echoed by flaring interest rates, inflation, and high unemployment.

Back in the summer of 1972, Lowe's stock price had hit $87. At the end of that fiscal year on July 31, the company reported earnings per share of $1.08, for a price-to-earnings ratio of eighty to one—a record high for Lowe's that has never been bettered. Then the clouds started rolling in. Housing starts plunged from an annual rate of over 2 million in August of 1972 to 1.1 million in August of 1974. Lowe's builder market was severely curtailed. As inflation and rising unemployment chipped away at real income and consumer confidence, Lowe's retail sales also began to suffer. In 1975, Lowe's reported its first decline in annual sales and earnings since the decade began.

Measures were taken: expansion plans were scaled back, budgets were cut, and new incentive programs and marketing strategies were generated. One of the latter was Lowe's "Un-flation" tabloid advertising, in which Lowe's reproduced ads from previous years to prove that in the case of many items, prices had actually decreased—at least at Lowe's.

By 1976, things were looking up. Retail sales were growing again, and contractor sales were recovering as the Sunbelt migration brought thousands of new residents to the Southeast.

However, seeds of doubt had been planted in many furrowed brows. The homebuilder business had brought Lowe's a long way, but maybe it was time to unhitch the wagon.

They shoot horses, don't they?

The Office of the President had guided Lowe's through five years of breathtaking change and growth. In 1970, Lowe's was a chain of 64 stores doing $128 million in total sales; by 1975, there were 141 stores and sales topped $388 million.

Joe Reinhardt had supervised the development of the Accusale store computer system, which was launched in 1974. Designed by John Acree, it replaced the old punch-card system with sales

In an era of inflation, Lowe's Un-flation campaign advertised items whose prices at Lowe's had actually gone down.

information stored on tape and transmitted to the general office over phone lines. Once again, Lowe's was in the technological vanguard of the retail industry.

However, there were other strains on the operational infrastructure. In 1975, a hairline crack appeared at store level, becoming a wide and deep crevasse by the time it reached the Office of the President. It all started when a report surfaced that store managers were having trouble getting products from the central warehouse.

"Pete's buyers would order merchandise and think 'Okay, that's taken care of,'" explains Bob Strickland. "Then a store manager would call a buyer to ask about an item, and the buyer would say 'We've got plenty—in the warehouse.' The store manager would say 'Well, I don't have any in my store, and I've been out for ten days.' And the buyer would say 'Well, it's been billed'—meaning that he had made out the order, and it had left his hands. The timing of the shipping of the bill, however, was up to Joe and his warehouse people. It could get pretty messy."

To put authority and accountability in the same hands, the Office of the President voted to give Pete Kulynych responsibility for the central warehouse as well as the purchasing. Joe Reinhardt was deeply offended. He didn't see the change as a move to rationalize procedures; he only knew that the other guys were taking the warehouse away from him.

He decided that he'd had enough. There was no doubt about it: the past few years at Lowe's had been exciting and demanding—exciting for Johnny Walker and his sales force, and demanding for people on Joe's side of the business. He was only human; his patience had run out, and it was time for him to leave.

"Two or three days later, Bill McElwee and I went to Joe's office," Leonard Herring says. "We closed the door and appealed to him personally, trying to talk him into staying, but it didn't work."

Joe Reinhardt retired in December of 1975. He had done a good job for the company; now he could enjoy the fruits of his labors. He retired a multimillionaire, and never needed to work again. He had been with Lowe's for nineteen years.

Lowe's Profit Sharing Plan had been making headlines since early in the decade, as long-time employees began to retire rich.

Byrnal Wade operates an Accusale store computer.

The plan's first millionaire was Hal Church, the only Lowe's employee with more seniority than Pete Kulynych. Hal had been part of Lowe's management for years; however, many of Lowe's successful retirees were warehousemen, truck drivers, lumber graders, and clerical workers.

The March 31, 1975 issue of *Newsweek* contained an article in the Business and Finance section titled "Lowe's Largesse." It cited the example of Lowe's employee Charles Valentine, a warehouse worker who never made more than $125 a week, but who retired with more than $660,000 from his profit sharing distribution.

The company puts aside an amount equal to 15 percent of an employee's salary each year on a store-by-store basis, if the store has met its profit goals; employees pay nothing into the fund. Ninety percent of the money is invested in Lowe's stock—and that's the secret. The stock has performed spectacularly since it went public at $12.25 a share in 1961. The value of that initial share is worth 25 times the offering price.

Ferrell Bryant, who drove a Lowe's delivery truck, retired at age 47 with $413,000. Fred Walters, who joined Lowe's at the Asheville store in 1953, retired in 1972 at age 44 with more than $2 million. Cecil Murray, Lowe's personnel manager, retired with $3.5 million at the age of fifty.

The early success stories passed swiftly into legend throughout Lowe's organization, and provided a powerful incentive to newer employees. Yet by the mid-Seventies, Bob Strickland began to think that the plan was looking a little anemic.

In 1971, the plan had sold some of its stock for cash liquidity. Retiring employees had also taken stock out of the plan. The result was that the plan's ownership of Lowe's stock had declined from 48 percent to 19 percent of the total shares outstanding. Meanwhile, Lowe's employee count had grown from 300 to 4,000.

As the average number of shares per plan member declined,

Sterling Advertising definitely had the Seventies look, as personified by H.C. Poythress and Claude Bullis.

employees began to realize that they might not have the same opportunity as those lucky ones who had gone before them. Consequently, the plan's incentive value began to weaken.

Few employers were as visionary as Carl Buchan. The Tax Reform Act of 1976 contained tax incentives designed to encourage companies less progressive than Lowe's to set up Employee Stock Ownership Plans (ESOP's) for their workers.

Under the terms of an ESOP, an employer annually contributes company stock (or cash to buy company stock) in exchange for a tax deduction in the amount of the contribution. The contributed stock is held in an escrow account for later allocation to individual employee accounts. Employees earn their stock ownership by sticking with the company until they are "vested" in the ESOP. When they leave or retire, they receive the portion of stock in their account to which they are entitled under the vesting schedule.

Lowe's Office of the President decided that ESOP's were the wave of the future, and that Lowe's should catch the wave. On December 31, 1977, membership in the old profit sharing plan was frozen; the new ESOP began on January 1, 1978. Members in the prior plan, who could decide how they wanted their share distributed, overwhelmingly chose to invest it in Lowe's stock rather than take it in cash.

Once again, Lowe's faith in its employees was equaled by their faith in Lowe's.

Ben Phillips on feeling the force:

"In the mid-Seventies, the pro business was going to hell in a hand basket. Housing starts were down, and Lowe's didn't have the retail business to compensate.

"John Walker would leave North Wilkesboro at five in the morning on an old Cessna 310 or 411. He'd go to some store and have breakfast with the employees before it opened, and at night he'd have dinner with employees at another store after the store had closed.

"He was carrying the banner for the company, trying to put some motivation back in the people. He was trying to get ordinary

Top: Nipper, the RCA dog, mesmerized by Lowe's logo on a console TV. The image appeared on the cover of a Lowe's quarterly report.
Bottom: This robot made guest appearances at Lowe's store openings. Operated by remote control, it greeted customers with relentless cheerfulness and never had a bad hair day.

Gimme an "L"
Gimme an "O"
Gimme a "W"
Gimme an "E"
Gimme an "Apostrophe"
Gimme an "S"

What's that spell?

Well, yes, of course it spells Lowe's. But to thousands of Lowe's employees in the Sixties and Seventies, it also spelled "hootenanny."

The standard definition of "hootenanny" is "an informal performance by folk artists." There was nothing standard about Lowe's hootenanny sales meetings, but they did feature performances by folk of all kinds—from Nashville's Roy Clark to Lowe's own Bob Strickland.

Hootenanny Saturday night was always pure fun, a celebration of the past year's success in an atmosphere of easy camaraderie. Sunday was for business: financial results and budgets for the new year were discussed, and new product lines were introduced. Best of all, new sales incentives were announced—everything from $25 bonuses to new cars and trips to Las Vegas, Hawaii, and Europe.

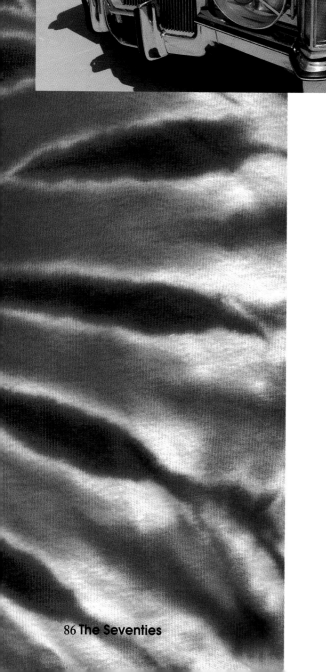

people to do extraordinary things. He did his best, and it was unbelievable what he could do."

Dick Griffin on not sweating the details:

"I was hired to run the leadership school, but ended up in charge of Installed Sales instead.

"One day not long after I got there, Walker called my office and said 'Okay, you've got fifteen minutes at the hootenanny on Sunday.' I asked 'What's a hootenanny?' He said 'Hasn't Dwight told you?' And he hung up the phone.

"Dwight came tearing into my office a minute later and said 'Look, at these hootenannies we bring in all the salesmen and all the store managers. John's giving you fifteen minutes on the program to talk about Installed Sales.'

"I said 'Hell, I don't know enough to talk about it yet.' But Dwight said 'Well, you've got to do something. Walker said to put you on.'

Top: **Custom Cadillac owned by Johnny Walker.**
Below: **Harvey Hackit, an endearing do-it-yourselfer, was created by Mike Willis and Henry Church of Sterling Advertising for a TV campaign.**

The Reluctant Handyman

"At the hootenanny, Walker's presentation was based on the word 'enthusiasm.' It was my turn next. He introduced me as 'the new fellow from Sears who's gonna take over Installed Sales and make it what it ought to be. Let's bring out, and give a big hand to, Dick RICHARDSON!'

"I thought, 'Who in the hell is Dick Richardson?' Then I was on."

Ross Burgess on knowing how to pick'em:

"Just think: Carl Buchan met Leonard forty years ago and saw that he had the capacity to do what he's done. He saw Strickland fresh from Harvard, and knew he could do it, too. He saw Walker— 'the hotshot,' he called him—and knew he could create the motivational atmosphere to make Lowe's the top sales organization in the country.

"Buchan never needed anybody but Walker to be sales manager. He never needed anybody but Reinhardt to be his operations man. Through all those years, Pete was responsible for purchasing and inventory and the turnover and margins, and Buchan never needed to replace him.

"It's remarkable. If you look until your eyes cross, you won't find another company that went public in 1961 in which so many of the first generation executives lasted through so much."

Top: A fisheye view of a Lowe's grand opening in the Seventies. Rome Christie was in charge of making sure there was always a balloon nozzle for the helium canisters. Bottom: For a while, Lowe's carried go-karts and Czechoslovakian-made JAWA motorcycles.

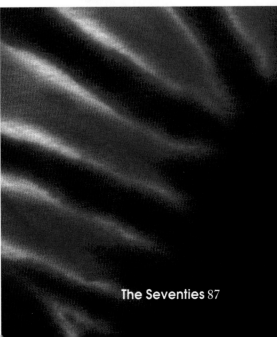

Each of the members of the Office of the President was the head of a departmental organization extending from entry level jobs all the way to the boardroom.

"Lowe's was running as five separate entrepreneurial companies within this building, and we met every Monday to tie things together," Leonard says. "Afterward, I would write the minutes and distribute them to everybody the next morning. We had to try to keep it focused."

"As the company grew," says Pete, "it got more difficult to make a decision for your department that didn't overlap someone else's. Sometimes you couldn't get hold of your counterpart to consult about it. Know what I mean? People were busy or they were traveling; it was hard not to miss the meetings."

Lowe's began 1978 with 180 stores and more than five thousand employees. "Yet there was only one person in the Personnel Department—and he had his hands full just running the payroll!" says Leonard.

"We had no internal audit department to check procedures. We had no formalized capital expenditure plan. Nobody had developed any functions that crossed departmental lines, because nobody really had the authority. No responsibility had been assigned for that. Nobody thought about it, and nobody had the time, anyway."

It was a measure of the success of the Office of the President that Lowe's had come so far, so quickly. But it was also undeniable that once again, the company had outgrown its management structure the way a healthy child outgrows its clothes. Lowe's could no longer be run by a committee. It was time for the board of directors to step in.

A management consulting firm called Diebold was hired to study the situation. It fell to Gordon Cadwgan, as an outside director and trusted friend of the Lowe's team, to take Diebold's findings into consideration and make a recommendation.

It was a tough decision—one that had never been made by

Beginning in 1979, Lowe's own credit card was added to other customer credit options.

Carl Buchan or by anyone in the 27 years since his death. Adding to the difficulty was the fact that John Walker thought the solution was obvious.

"Walker and I talked," says Gordon, "and he told me that he was entitled to be Lowe's president and chairman because he had contributed the most to building the company.

"Johnny was a genius as a sales manager. He was full of fun, and he loved a good time, but sometimes he went a little too far." He also was an aggressive self-promoter who had never hidden his personal ambition. It was all part of the Johnny Walker package; however, Carl Buchan himself had begun Lowe's tradition of selecting its management's virtues *a la carte*. By pushing his claim to the top spot, Walker had made himself more a part of the problem than part of the solution.

"I talked to all the members of the team," Gordon recalls. "Finally, I was ready to report to the board."

A board meeting was held in Washington, D.C. in July of 1978. At that meeting, Gordon recommended that both John Walker and Pete Kulynych be made managing directors, active on the board but no longer responsible for management decisions on a daily basis.

"I was feeling burned out, and I was willing to step aside," says Pete. "Johnny didn't want to, but it helped that someone else was going besides him—and I was the oldest."

At that point, Gordon suggested that Lowe's defy convention once again. Instead of choosing one man to be both CEO and chairman, he recommended that Leonard Herring be named president and chief executive officer, and that Bob Strickland become Lowe's chairman of the board.

"Leonard was the hands-on, day-to-day operating man, respected as a natural leader," Gordon explains. "Bob had vision, with a different orientation: he was more likely to wake up in the middle of the night, thinking about Lowe's long-term future.

"Not too long after, Met Life did the same thing: they made Bob Schwartz chairman and someone else president and CEO. At some point during this process, John Diebold himself brought out a report on this new, efficient way of handling things!"

Rail transport was still important to Lowe's. Here, the expansion team (left to right) of George Hart, Kenny Brooks, Lin Brooks, Brian Robbins, and Wade Dupree see how close to the tracks Lowe's can get.

Lowe's reorganization announcement met with varying degrees of surprise and understanding in the stores and the general office.

"It was a surprise, but it made sense," says Dwight Pardue. "Leonard was the one who always kept his cool."

Ross Burgess agrees. "I'd always had to be flexible with Johnny, because he could change his mind between the time he left my store and the time he got back to the general office. But I never encountered that with Leonard. Once he told me something, it was in concrete. If he said 'Ross, we can do this,' I never looked back; if he said 'Ross, we can't do that,' I never questioned it. That was a great way to work."

Frank Beam was Store Manager of the Year in 1978. Remembering the reorganization, he says "Some people had thought John might be made president because of his sales background. But for running the corporation, we needed an all-around, balanced leader. Once Leonard became president, Lowe's was on its way."

– – –

Top: Rome Christie opened 362 stores for Lowe's. Everybody knew things were ready to go when Rome put "Yackety Sax" on the public address system.
Bottom: Lowe's was welcomed into new markets such as Columbus, Georgia, where the local Holiday Inn extended a greeting.

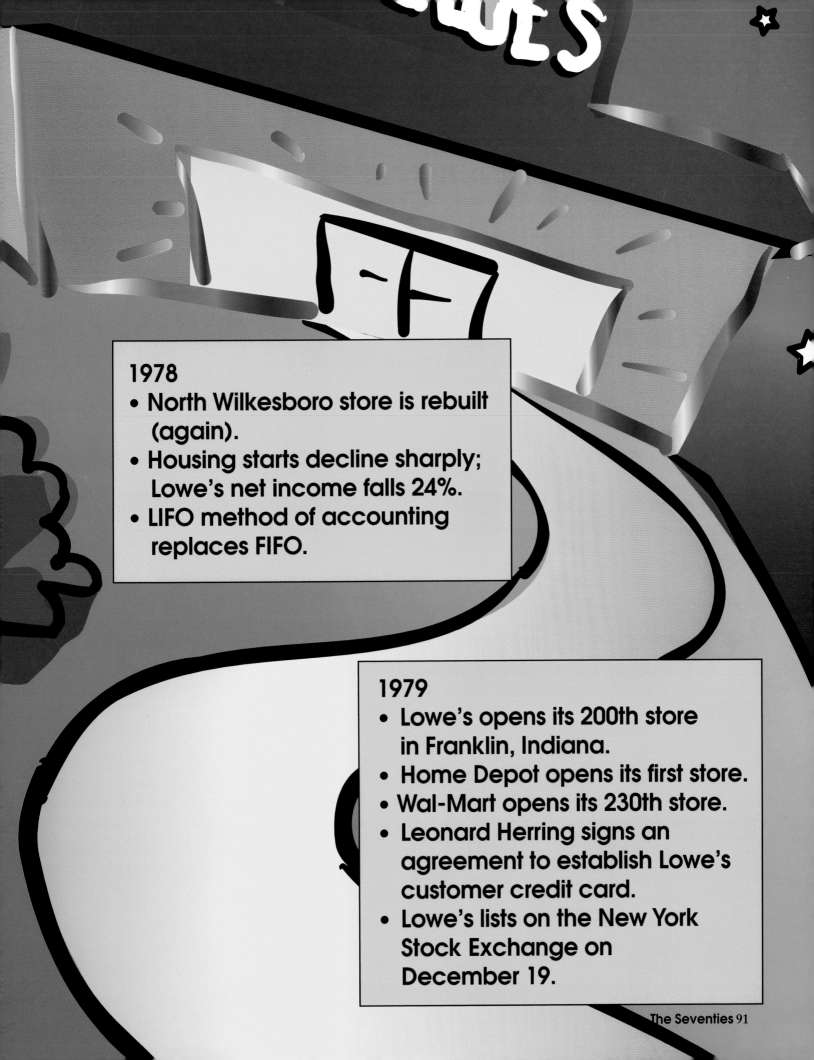

1978

- North Wilkesboro store is rebuilt (again).
- Housing starts decline sharply; Lowe's net income falls 24%.
- LIFO method of accounting replaces FIFO.

1979

- Lowe's opens its 200th store in Franklin, Indiana.
- Home Depot opens its first store.
- Wal-Mart opens its 230th store.
- Leonard Herring signs an agreement to establish Lowe's customer credit card.
- Lowe's lists on the New York Stock Exchange on December 19.

The Eighties

"First impressions? The lobby at Lowe's headquarters was a tiny waiting room with plastic chairs. There was one receptionist. Everybody was on a first-name basis. It wasn't a corporate atmosphere that immediately screamed 'baby blue chip company.' But the people I met there could have gone anywhere, done anything. I saw what they had achieved since going public, and what they were planning to do next, and I was excited by the opportunity."

— Greg Bridgeford

The reorganized Lowe's began the new decade in an economic environment that badly needed some reorganization itself. Throughout the late Seventies, inflation and interest rates had climbed steadily. The expenses of daily life consumed larger and larger portions of middle America's household income, leaving the United States with a savings rate only half that achieved by the rest of the developed world. Looking for higher returns on lower savings, consumers began to invest in money market funds and other financial instruments that promised attractive yields. Traditional savings institutions suffered, and so did the housing industry which they largely financed.

Since 1971, the price of a new home had doubled. Now mortgage rates surged in response to demand for diminished funds, putting homes out of reach of many potential buyers. The rate of housing starts tumbled, even in the Sunbelt. One month in 1980, there were so few housing starts in one of Lowe's markets that Bill Brantley, Lowe's vice president for investor relations, quipped "We don't count them anymore; we *name* them!"

Fortunately for Lowe's, reorganization had paved the way for a strategic change of direction. John Walker had always believed that Lowe's destiny lay with professional builders. During his heyday, the retail side of Lowe's business struggled for attention and resources, and its importance was only acknowledged when the housing indus-

Dwight Pardue carried the ball for Lowe's store operations staff as the Eighties began.

try took a downturn. By the late Seventies, very few people remembered that Lowe's had started out as a mass merchandiser to the general public, not as a lumber yard for builders.

"John was a salesman," says Bob Strickland. "Deep in his heart, he would have loved to sell the Brooklyn Bridge or the Graf Zeppelin. The bigger the ticket, the more he loved it."

Lowe's salespeople, who worked on commission, could hardly be blamed for feeling the same way.

"They made their money on volume," says Bob Tillman. "Retail customers were regarded as a nuisance. If you're writing up a $5,000 order for a builder, and some 'stick picker' comes in looking for $22 worth of lumber, who are you going to focus on?"

Lowe's made the most of its "pro" business when the housing industry was booming. But by the late Seventies, the years of two million housing starts were clearly over. With reorganization, Bob Strickland was given responsibility for long-range planning as well as shareholder and external relations. He didn't share Walker's builder bias; clearly, the time had come to get serious about retail sales.

In the 1978 annual report, Lowe's committed itself to achieving a 50/50 relationship between contractor sales and retail. Lowe's sales mix was currently 60/40. The implications of the proposed shift were more profound than numbers can convey.

"The biggest difference was the nature of retail itself," Leonard Herring explains. "I call the builder business a 'pull' business, and retail a 'push' business. To serve builders, Lowe's really didn't need merchants; we just needed purchasing people to make sure that Lowe's always had whatever the builders needed to pull from our stores. The job of our sales force was to develop and maintain relationships with those builders, so that they would continue to 'pull' from Lowe's.

"Retail is entirely different: it's a 'push' business. As a retailer, Lowe's has to be a merchant. We not only provide the box full of products; we also have to stimulate desire for the products we carry. We have to have the right pricing, advertising, and display. We have to serve a much wider variety of customers, and we have to 'push' the products to them.

"In 1978, the size and layout of our stores, our business hours, even the way our salespeople were compensated—all reflected the influence of the builders who were our dominant customer group," Leonard says. "Our sales floors were set up like catalogue showrooms, with 'one to show and one to go.' The sales floors were small—sometimes just five or six thousand square feet. Customers had to drive around back to pick up whatever they bought. You made out a ticket so the customer could drive around and pick up a television."

Late in 1978, with housing starts circling the drain and Lowe's just settling into its new management structure, Leonard had received an unsolicited offer from an Atlanta-based design firm, Miller/Zell, to update its layout and image.

"I asked Mike Brown, who was in charge of our marketing services, to invite Miller/Zell to send someone to call on us. The person they sent was Steve Herman, a retail consultant out of Boston. We had a couple of meetings and Bob Strickland got into it, liked what he heard, and the whole thing picked up steam."

Herman's basic idea was to make Lowe's stores into better retail vehicles.

"We were standing together in the North Wilkesboro store with Larry Stone, who was the manager,"

Lowe's specialists in real estate and store design had big plans for enlarging the future of Lowe's.

Bob recalls. "Steve asked, 'How do people shop this store?' and Larry said 'Well, they come in and browse around until they see what they want.' And Steve said 'I mean, what are their traffic patterns?' And we didn't have a clue.

"Then Steve said 'I'll bet you ten dollars that seven out of the next ten people who come through the front door will turn here, go down this aisle, and head into the hardware gondolas.' That was our most popular department at the time. And he was right!"

Herman advised Lowe's to organize its products according to their gender-based appeal—to put the things that women buy on one side of the store, and things that men buy on the other side. He developed a U-shaped arrangement that would invite customers down one side, around the middle, and up the other side to the checkout. That way they wouldn't miss anything Lowe's had to offer.

"Another important part of the scheme was what we called the 'Four Corners' strategy [after Chapel Hill basketball coach Dean Smith's infamously effective delaying offense]. What we had in the four corners were categories grouped by big-ticket project types: cabinets and paint, lighting, millwork and building materials, appliances and electronics.

"It made sense to get people out of the traffic flow in those areas, because they needed to take their time," Bob explains.

Finally, Herman advised Lowe's to open up store

warehouses and give consumers access to that area as well. Miller/Zell helped Lowe's brighten the look of its stores with new signs and banners. The whole package was implemented at Lowe's North Charlotte store, which opened in January of 1980. Despite the ambient economic malaise, it posted some of the best sales results in the history of new Lowe's stores.

Bob Strickland christened the Miller/Zell treatment "RSVP" for Retail Sales Volume and Profit. During 1980,

seventeen stores were RSVP "retrofitted," and another hundred were scheduled for the treatment.

RSVP was a signal to Lowe's sales force that the company was serious about its new focus on retail sales. It would be a gross understatement to say that not everyone was thrilled by the change.

"You wouldn't believe the agony," Leonard declares.

Lowe's checkout during a grand opening.

"Some people got on board right away, even though they may not have had any retailing experience. But many were afraid that there wouldn't be a place for them in the New Lowe's."

Larry Stone:

"I did a lot of builder business, but I was always intrigued by the retail side. I was fascinated by the number of lawn mowers and appliances I could sell on a Saturday.

"I went straight from being a retail sales manager to being a store manager, just as Lowe's was beginning to concentrate on retail business. I'd go to managers' meetings and listen to guys who didn't want to give up the builder orientation. They'd say 'We'll have merchandise returns, we'll have more customer complaints—' and I'd always say 'Yes, but we'll make a lot more money.'

"I said 'If a customer has a problem with merchandise, just take it back.' And they said 'You're crazier than hell.'"

Ben Phillips:

"A tradition had been built around serving the contractor customer. RSVP was a cultural challenge to that tradition. Going for retail changed the style of Lowe's operation. It became less entrepreneurial and more formal, more function-oriented.

"My interest was always the professional builder business. I had to struggle to concentrate on the front door. It made me something of a black sheep in the family: I kept fighting to keep the contractor business in the forefront.

"I felt I was waving the flag for contractors, but I was a parade of one. I said 'I am your leader'—and I looked

Lowe's merchandising staff at the National Home Center Show in Chicago.

around, and nobody was behind me."

Frank Beam:

"I was for making money. It made no difference to me whether it was retail or contractor money. My goal was to make a profit for the store.

"Sure, it was hard for all of us who grew up in the contractor business to make that shift. But we saw where the money was being made.

"If Lowe's hadn't changed, we'd be out of business today, or just doing so-so. There have been too many ups and downs, too many bad times for the housing industry. It takes a lot of capital to finance builders' accounts receivable.

"In the builder business, the margin is always lower. It's partly a function of the commodity products involved; then there are the delivery trucks and delivery labor, accounts receivable and bad debts.

"The builder business was about relationships. Retail is not as much about relationships as it is about having great products, great service, and a great shopping environment."

Ross Burgess:

"We had to stop being a lumber yard for the builder and start being a viable source of products for the consumer—and that was one heck of a lot harder to do than it is to say."

Bill Brantley:

"RSVP caught the fancy of Wall Street. We started printing what the retail square footage was going to be, and the Street started paying attention to Lowe's again, although housing starts were still incredibly low and didn't start picking up until 1983."

Leonard Herring recalls that the most difficult decision he's had to make as president was in 1981, when he decided to start opening Lowe's stores on Sundays.

"It was part of the transition to retail," he says.

Top: Selling lumber to retail customers in the Eighties.
Bottom: By the mid-Eighties, Lowe's 7,400-square-foot store in Wilson, NC had outgrown both its size and location.

"But it was a very tough call to make.

"Ray Ferguson was managing our store in Hendersonville, North Carolina. For a while, he was one of the few active employees who had longer service with Lowe's than I had.

"Ray came to see me and said that he could not work on Sunday. I told him I was very sorry, and I hoped he could find a way to accommodate the decision, but I couldn't back down. I certainly understood his position, but the decision had been necessary.

"Well, I think everyone in Ray's church wrote me a letter or called me after that, including the pastor. But we opened on Sunday anyway. And on the second or third Sunday that we were open, the pastor's pipes froze and he was *in our store!*

"I never heard another word about it."

During the recession of 1980-81, Lowe's retail business increased sixteen percent. In 1981, for the first time in twenty years, retail sales surpassed contractor sales. Lowe's had achieved its goal of a 50/50 sales mix.

Since Lowe's initial stock offering in 1961, there had been several stock splits and dividends. In 1981, the stock again split three-for-two, in effect increasing each stockholder's number of shares by fifty percent. The number of shares authorized was also increased from twenty million to fifty million.

Lowe's had been listed on the New York Stock Exchange since 1979. Starting in January of 1981, it was also traded on the Pacific Exchange in San Francisco. In an effort to further broaden the base of Lowe's ownership and provide both for growth and for stock price stability, the company now looked for savvy new investors in Europe. The Stock

Bob Strickland talks to investor Farrokh Deboo in Lowe's Asheville store.

Exchange in London was selected as the most promising marketplace, and trading in Lowe's stock was begun there on October 6, 1981.

In the 1981 annual report, the letter to shareholders from Bob Strickland and Leonard Herring was translated into German, Dutch, French, Spanish, Japanese, and Arabic. It was a salute to Lowe's international investors—and it made the point (not too subtly for impact) that Lowe's was thinking globally. Tokyo, Riyadh, Edinburgh—and North Wilkesboro? You could get there from here.

The soaring cost of home construction in the inflationary Seventies spurred rapid growth in the size of the do-it-yourself market and in the number of retailers who were attracted to it. By the early Eighties, "building supply retailing" had become a hot sector, and an increasing number of regional chains were staking claims.

Payless Cashways was a publicly held chain of 130 home centers headquartered in Kansas City and capably run by a former investment banker and lawyer named David Stanley. Hechinger was a chain of forty large stores based in Landover, Maryland and run by John Hechinger, the son of founder Sidney.

Evans Products encompassed the Grossman's, Lindsley, and Moore's chains, and was run by the controversial corporate raider, Victor Posner. Wickes operated some 300 stores from its headquarters in Santa Monica, California, and by 1983 was already undergoing the first of its reorganizations under Chapter 11 bankruptcy protection.

Then there was Home Depot, which had been just a blip on Lowe's radar screen in 1979. The brainchild of innovative retailer Bernie Marcus, in 1983 it was still a small chain of very large warehouse stores primarily in urban markets. The conventional wisdom at Lowe's discounted its potential as serious competition, in the belief that the warehouse concept would either fail or restrict the Home Depot to big cities.

"I remember my first exposure to the Home Depot," Bob Tillman says. "Lowe's had a store managers' meeting in Orlando in 1981, and we made time to visit Home Depot's store there.

"The store was 85,000 square feet. We were on a little bus, and we could not find an empty space in the parking lot. Leonard was with us, and he said 'I'll bet you could sell these parking spaces for $5 apiece.' At that moment, I knew they had built a better mousetrap—before we ever went into the store!

"I had always loved the retail business. I grew up in retail. My grandfather owned a store in Mount Olive—Henry Tillman's General Mercantile.

"In Wilmington, our Lowe's store was already doing high volume in retail. RSVP could finetune and enhance the product selection, but we were limited by our 11,000-square-foot store. We needed a bigger store. We needed space for more products. RSVP couldn't solve that problem. It couldn't take us where we wanted to go.

"I saw Bob Strickland in the spring of 1982 at a race in Charlotte, and I laid out what I wanted to do, which was to more than double the size of our store from 11,000 to

For a while, Lowe's referred to big-ticket consumer durables as one of its "three businesses," along with retail and contractor sales.

24,000 square feet. I sketched my idea on a cocktail napkin. Bob said 'Write this up and send it to Leonard, and I'll support you.'

"That conversation was a catalyst for me. I drew my idea more or less to scale, and put in a formal request for the capital that would be required, which was about $720,000. I told Leonard that if he okayed this 'super-retrofit,' the store would make $2 million in pre-tax profit in the first year.

"The retrofit was done exactly to my plan. It was finished early in 1984, and all the retail analysts came there for their spring meeting.

"The guys in store merchandising—Bill Pelon, Teddy Huddler, and the rest—were very cooperative about adding items and expanding lines for us. We would talk about plumbing and electrical—what customers wanted that we didn't have. We added products across a lot of categories, and it worked out great.

"We put in the first lawn and garden department as an experiment. We bought a lot locally—plants, grass, sod. We

bought fertilizer from a local fertilizer plant. The store did a lot of sourcing: I'd say 'I want to carry this brand of shingles, I want this kind of stud, I want my pressure-treated lumber from this Regal Paper plant.' And I'd be issued a purchase order. So although we had central buying, the store had a lot of input and autonomy as well.

To celebrate the launch of Lowe's first super-retrofitted store in Wilmington, NC, analysts were entertained aboard the battleship U.S.S. North Carolina.

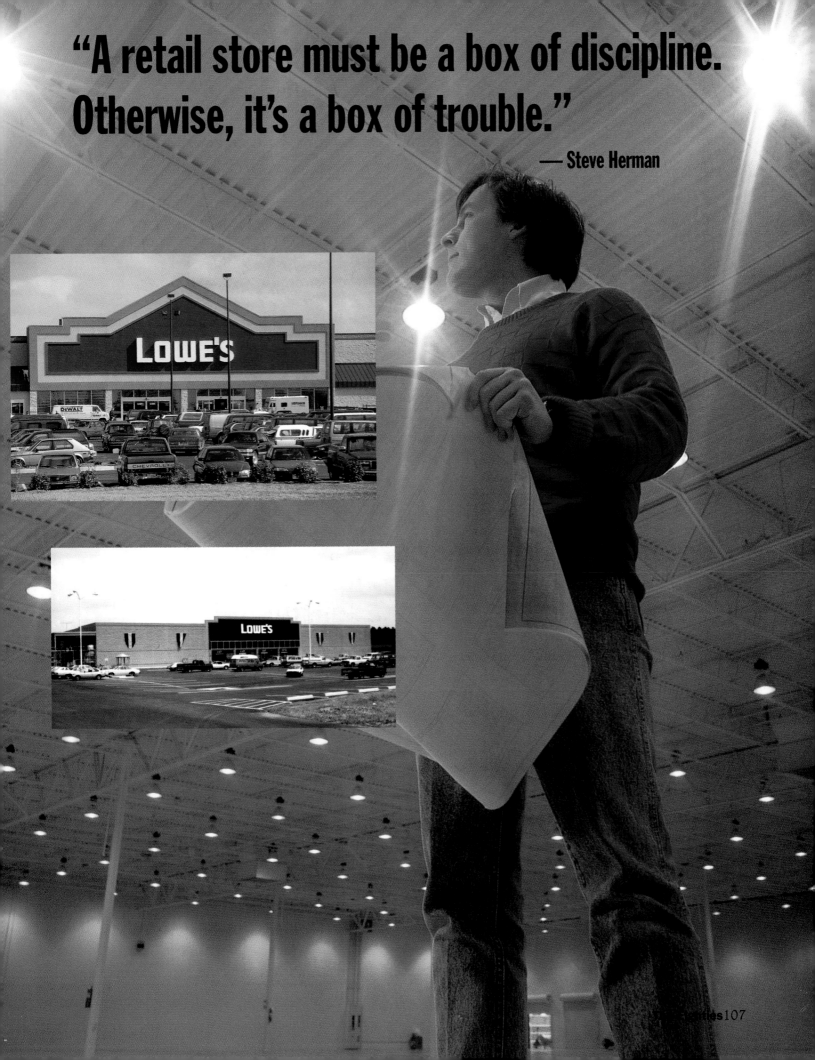

"A retail store must be a box of discipline. Otherwise, it's a box of trouble."

— Steve Herman

"The basic rule was that if you were going to take a chance, you promised to make good—and then you had to follow through. I promised Leonard Herring that in the first year after the super-retrofit, we would do $2 million in pre-tax profits. Then suddenly we were eight months into the year, and we had only made $1 million.

"In the last four months of that year, our store made a million dollars. We made $250,000 in pre-tax profits for four months in a row. It was a gigantic amount. Leonard brought it up in a board meeting, saying that our store had made $10,000 in profits *every day* for the last four months of the year.

"You lived or died by your credibility. And it was the same with the purchasing group. If you told them to buy something for your store, you made damn sure you sold it—even if it meant going door-to-door! Because you needed their cooperation to get the merchandise you wanted."

Although he approached the question from a different angle than Bob Tillman, Ross Burgess arrived at a similar conclusion: RSVP was an improvement, but not a solution. Lowe's needed bigger sales floors.

"I remember when conversations in meetings began to get serious about expanding the size of Lowe's sales floors," he says. "Bob Strickland had a vision of what we

Top: A Lowe's truck on a state highway near North Wilkesboro.
Bottom: In 1986, Lowe's distribution center in Villa Rica, Georgia was brand new and state-of-the-art at 397,000 square feet. In 1996, it has been outgrown.

Lowe's billboards in the 1980's were some of the best roadside advertising since Burma Shave. For these award-winning achievements, Steve Huggins of Sterling Advertising was dubbed "king of the one-liners."

Left, the Pink Panther, star of movies and animated cartoons, hired on as spokesman for Owens Corning and was used widely in Lowe's print advertising when the price of energy turned consumer attention to energy conservation through insulation.

Below, Bob Strickland takes on Pac-Man. When Lowe's sold Atari video games, this prototype of computer-game protagonists (Pac-Man, not Strickland) was the focus of marketing promotions.

could do with a 50,000-square-foot store. He asked Ralph Buchan and me to go to our North Wilkesboro store together, to look at what was displayed and how it was displayed, and to come back and tell him how much space I thought we really needed to properly merchandise that product line.

"I'll never forget going down there with a tape measure, a yellow pad, and Ralph. We went over every inch of that store. I believe the number we came up with was 22,000 square feet.

"I took that number back to the general office, and you would think I had driven a tank through the front of the store. Everybody was saying *'Twenty-two thousand feet?!'* They were shocked. They said 'How in the world would you display it?' Hell, I didn't know. All I knew was that if we wanted to show the right amount of hardware and paint and plumbing, that's the space we needed.

"We hashed it out and decided to expand Lowe's sales floors, and to expand the product lines, and to figure out how best to do this when some of our sales floors were 8,000 square feet while others were 10,000, others were 12,500, and others were 17,000!

"I remember conversations with Bob about the big stores in Lowe's future. I remember conversations with Leonard about how to expand the product lines and manage the inventories and still keep the company financially sound.

Ah, the new Lowe's! And the new new Lowe's. Or was this the *new* new new Lowe's? Lowe's stores went through so many changes in the Eighties that management took considerable good-natured ribbing. Customer response, however, made it more than worthwhile.

"Leonard was very supportive, but he was responsible for Lowe's net after tax, and he realized that the builder was, as the old saying goes, 'the one that brought us to the dance.'"

In 1982, Lowe's had its first billion-dollar sales year and earned a record $25.1 million. The following year was (finally) a good one for the housing industry, and Lowe's contractor sales jumped 53 percent. Retail sales grew by 27 percent, for an overall sales increase of 38 percent.

In 1982, Lowe's earnings topped $50 million for the first time. Since then, the company has never earned less than $50 million a year.*

"I'm as proud of that as of anything that we achieved during my presidency," says Leonard Herring.

"'Six million per store by '84'—that was our slogan," Bob Strickland recalls. "We had done about $2 million in annual sales per store all through the Seventies: $1.4 million in contractor sales, and $.6 million in retail. So it was a big leap to aim for $3 million in retail sales per store, fueled by RSVP.

"We actually achieved it in 1983, a year early. But we realized that we were bumping our noses in our smaller stores. Although 11,000 square feet had been our standard size until then, in the spring of 1984 we announced that henceforth, all Lowe's new stores would be at least 20,000 square feet."

In September of 1984, John Walker died of a heart attack after rushing down to Holden Beach to rescue his wife, Beryl, from the fury of Hurricane Diana.

David Shelton had known Johnny since 1970. "I will always remember him talking about Lowe's nobility of purpose," he says. "I found it inspiring to hear that we not only have jobs, we're also providing a service to people in our communities.

* The technical exception was 1991, when a restructuring charge of $71.3 million was taken for future expansion.

"It *is* meaningful work to help people build and repair their homes. Lowe's nobility of purpose is one reason I love this company—and that's part of Johnny Walker's legacy."

It was the decade of leveraged buyouts, of mergers and acquisitions. In the Eighties, if you weren't a predator, you were prey—and it was not uncommon to be both at once.

"Lowe's was interested in acquisitions at the time," says Greg Bridgeford, who joined the company as Bob Strickland's administrative assistant in 1982. "It was seen as a quick way to gain market share in good operating locations.

"We had capital and strong cash flow. Instead of going into new markets and wearing down a competitor, why not just buy him out?

"In the Seventies, Lowe's bought single stores. In the Eighties, we looked at small chains. We looked at Moore-Handley, based in Birmingham, and bought three of their stores. We looked at a lot of chains, but usually ended up buying just a couple of locations. Rarely was the match just right in terms of store size, location, and market type. There were a lot of stores on the market, though—lots of opportunities, because times were tough.

"At one time or another during the Eighties, almost every chain was on the block. Some were bought, some went under, and survivors purchased the assets of those who had failed. But there wasn't a whole lot of value created. None of them had an operating format that created long-term value for shareholders."

In 1985, Lowe's purchased 23 stores from Boise Cascade's Building Materials Distribution Division. Eight of the stores were in the Dallas / Fort Worth area, nine were in smaller towns in central and northeastern Texas, and the rest were in Oklahoma. The stores were builder-oriented, as Lowe's stores were before RSVP; their sales floors averaged about the same size as Lowe's; their average annual sales per store were about the same as Lowe's, and in 1984, *every single one* made a profit. All they needed was a little TLC and RSVP to turn them into model Lowe's stores and carry Lowe's banner into a new—and famously prosperous—part of the country.

The price, after some negotiating, had been very attractive. It seemed like the perfect match. During 1985, the stores were stocked with a basic assortment of Lowe's product lines. They were equipped with Lowe's in-store computers, and scheduled for RSVP makeovers.

The outbreak of war between Iran and Iraq in 1980 had boosted oil prices to record highs. At the beginning of 1981, the price of crude oil was nineteen times what it had been ten years earlier. The price of oil was a major cause of the worldwide recession which had gotten the Eighties off to such a glum start. It did, however, promote energy conservation.

Demand for oil slackened as alternatives were explored. At the same time, oil from non-OPEC areas such as the North Sea, Mexico, Brazil, and China began to increase the available supply. The world oil market slumped, taking the economy of the oil patch with it. In little more than a year, the contractor-oriented stores of Lowe's Boise Cascade acquisition lost fifty percent of their contractor sales volume.

Illustration by Bruce Tucker

For a while, Lowe's put a good face on the misfortune, hoping that the downturn would be brief. However, by 1987 the stores were deemed "consistently unprofitable" and were closed. In addition to operating losses, the company took a charge of $9.8 million to cover closing costs.

"Many people in Lowe's management were disappointed that the company's largest acquisition had been a failure," says Cliff Oxford, who joined Lowe's as director of in-

Lowe's executives on the floor of The Stock Exchange in London. Lowe's stock has been traded there since October 6, 1981.

vestor relations in 1984, just before the Boise deal was made. "But in fact, it was a wonderful investment in education.

"The $9.8 million write-off was less than the cost of one Lowe's store in 1996," Cliff continues. "The experience soured Lowe's appetite for any further acquisitions, and may have kept us from making a much bigger mistake somewhere else.

"It taught us to focus on opportunities in our existing markets, and to store up our base at a time when our competition was sending scouting parties into Lowe's Heartland. Because of the Boise Cascade experience, we got out of the mergers-and-acquisitions mindset of the Eighties and turned our attention toward developing a Lowe's store that would take us into the Nineties."

1983 - Pete Kulynych retires, but continues as administrator of Lowe's Charitable and Educational Foundation.

1984 - Lowe's is included in *The 100 Best Companies To Work For In America*, a popular book by Robert Levering and Milton Moskowitz.

1985 - IBM Series 1 computers are installed in 35 stores: Accusale is phased out.

1986 - Lowe's annual report wins the Gold Oscar from *Financial World.*

While Leonard Herring was managing Lowe's progress through the change and growth of the mid-Eighties, one of Bob Strickland's goals was to add to the breadth and depth of expertise that Lowe's board of directors had always

Bob Strickland and Cliff Oxford accept *Financial World's* Gold Oscar for the nation's best annual report in 1986.

represented. Everyone on the board—Bob and Leonard, Pete, Gordon Cadwgan, Bill McElwee, and Bob Schwartz—agreed that Lowe's board should seek some new members with retail experience.

Bob began recruiting. And since Lowe's is, after all, a North Carolina company, it was only fitting that two of the new recruits should be former basketball players.

Jack Shewmaker was born in Buffalo, Missouri and played basketball first at Buffalo High, then at Georgia Tech. After college he worked for Kroger and Coast-to-Coast Stores before joining a small but growing discount chain based in Bentonville, Arkansas.

Jack Shewmaker

In 1970, there were eighteen Wal-Marts and some variety stores in Sam Walton's chain. Jack started as a district manager; he was promoted several times over the next decade or so, eventually becoming Wal-Mart's president and chief operating officer, then vice chairman and chief financial officer. He was a member of Wal-Mart's board and also a member of the company's executive committee when he agreed to join Lowe's board of directors.

"There are quite a lot of similarities between Lowe's and Wal-Mart," Jack says. "The small town attitude is one. Another is that when you serve small communities, you can bring products in small quantities to small shipping docks. Your distribution facilities must be engineered to support smaller stores with regional warehousing: that keeps small stores in stock. Of course, to do this you must also have state-of-the-art technology. That's something that both Lowe's and Wal-Mart did.

"Lowe's put money where it was needed the most. First into its ESOP—to bring and retain good people. Second, Lowe's invested in small town America. Third, it invested in the state-of-the-art technology necessary for efficient regional distribution.

"Of course, the most important thing is to have a group of people who are willing to work hard together for a common goal, and to have fun doing it."

Lowe's other basketball-playing recruit was John Belk, whose father founded the Belk department store organization. In 1986, there were more than 360 Belk stores throughout the Southeast.

John grew up in Charlotte and played round ball for nearby Davidson College. Following a tour of active duty in Korea, he returned to Charlotte to work in the family business. Always active in civic affairs, he was eventually elected mayor of Charlotte and proved extremely popular, holding the office for a record four terms.

He is an Eagle Scout who has been in scouting all his life. When he took a seat on Lowe's board in 1986, he was the chairman of Belk Store Services and president of Belk Brothers Company.

"Belk began as a piece goods store in the small town of Monroe, North Carolina," he says. "That was in 1888.

"If you want long-term success, you've got to have good people. Belk had good people, and still does. So does Lowe's."

William Andres didn't play basketball, and it was basketball's loss. Andres was a native of Iowa who graduated from Upper Iowa University just in time to be shipped to Germany in 1944. After being discharged, he earned a graduate degree in retailing from the University of Pittsburgh, then went back to Iowa and took a

John Belk

Bill Andres

job with a retailer in Davenport.

In 1958 he went to work for Dayton Hudson Corporation, the national retailing giant which comprises the Target, Mervyn's, Dayton Hudson, and Lechmere chains. After working his way up through the ranks, he became chairman of the board. He had recently retired when Lowe's invited him to join its board in 1986.

Lowe's final new recruit was neither a basketball player nor a retailer. He was Senator Russell Long of Louisiana, son of Huey P. Long, the legendary populist who had been governor and senator in Louisiana before his assassination in 1935.

Senator Russell Long

Russell Long was president of the student body at Louisiana State and went on to get a law degree. Then he joined the Navy and saw active duty in the World War II invasions of Africa, Italy, and France. He was elected to the U.S. Senate one day before his thirtieth birthday in 1948. On Capitol Hill he became known for his keen debating skills, his knowledge of Senate rules, and his sense of humor.

He was chairman of the Senate Finance Committee for the better part of two decades, during which he became the leading Congressional champion of Employee Stock Ownership Plans. Several times, Bob Strickland had been called to Capitol Hill to testify before Congress on the value and virtues of Lowe's ESOP, and the two men had struck up a friendship. The senator's wife, Carolyn, is a Tarheel from Yanceyville who used to work for Senator Sam Ervin. Russell Long was elected to Lowe's board in 1987.

From first to last, it was an impressive recruiting class. Now Lowe's board was more than qualified to give whatever guidance the company needed as it moved into the next decade—and toward the next millennium.

Between Bob Tillman's first super-retrofit in Wilmington and Lowe's first 100,000-square-foot store, there were enough incremental steps and store prototypes to confuse anyone who didn't actually have to find the break room in each of them. However, you can't confuse Greg Bridgeford; he was there.

"They're tattooed on my brain," he admits. "Are you ready? Okay, here goes. In 1984, we had Douglasville, Georgia: that was 20,625 square feet. Then in 1985, there was the Kingsport, Tennessee prototype, with 27,000 square feet.

"Our 30,125-square-foot prototype was launched in 1986: Panama City, Florida was one of those. Also, in 1987 we had a prototype family: a 16,500 (Lenoir, NC, for example); a 26,400 (as in Waynesville, NC); and the 33,000-square-footer that we opened in North Tallahassee.

Top: Merchandising strategists and store operations vice presidents met regularly to coordinate growth objectives.
Bottom: A lighting display in the late Eighties.

"In 1989, our new Boone store was the first to have 45,000 square feet. In May of 1989, Goldsboro was the first with 65,000 feet. The 65,000-foot West Asheville store opened in June, and we held the board meeting in Asheville so all the directors could see it.

"Finally, there was Crown Point in Charlotte, which opened in 1990 with 95,000 square feet. We called it our first 100,000-square-foot store, but the merchandise assortment wasn't much wider than in West Asheville—only 25,000 sku's [stock-keeping units].

"Would you like me to get into sku count? No—I'll leave that to Tillman!"

Top: The front of Lowe's store in Boone, NC.
Bottom: Overhead view of Lowe's checkout area in 1989.

As Lowe's stores got larger, Lowe's product offering had to grow along with them. Layouts were refined, signage and pricing were improved, the technology of checkout and inventory systems was upgraded, and new ad campaigns were created.

By the end of the decade, there were 306 Lowe's stores in twenty states. Since 1980, Lowe's total sales floor had grown from less than two million square feet to more than six million. Lowe's employee family had increased from six thousand to more than fifteen thousand.

Lowe's 1989 sales were more than $2.6 billion, of which 62 percent was retail. Lowe's was indeed a retailer. Carl Buchan would not have believed the effort it took to make that happen.

Or maybe he would.

Photo illustration
by Henry Church & Will McIntyre

The Nineties

We have the desire to achieve dominance... we shall not be satisfied with anything less. The future of Lowe's and its people will be spectacularly fabulous.

— Carl Buchan

It's five a.m. in Lowe's Region One: time to wake up and smell the competition. Bill White is ready: let the Games begin! In his twenty years as Region One vice president, there has never been a time that he has enjoyed as much as this. "The next five years," he says, "will be the most exciting yet. We've got the right stores, the right programs, and the right people."

He wasn't always so confident. "A few years ago, we were sitting here with small stores, and along came HQ. Now we have our 'big box' stores with 40,000 sku's. The playing ground is level, and we're starting to take back business."

During the night, a freight truck has arrived at Lowe's Virginia Beach store from the new distribution center in Statesville. At five in the morning, the stocking team hits the sales floor. The merchandise was counted at the d.c., so all they have to do is put everything in its place. Their goal is to have all the freight cartons unloaded and shelved by ten o'clock, "so that the sales force can concentrate on serving the customer instead of working all day just to put up freight.

"Competition today is about having the right people in the right places at the right time," Bill says. "We have employees who work only in specific departments, such as Tool World or the garden center; we have dedicated cashiers and loaders whose job is to float the customers through checkout and departure.

"We've had call buttons in the aisles since about 1989, so that customers can push a button if they need service. For the

---

The Gregs of Merchandising: Wessling (left) and Bridgeford.

first few years, the usual response was that an employee would just run over and turn the button off! Another customer would hit the button . . . and so on. Then we got smart and said 'Hey, let's actually assist these folks!'

"Now in our large stores there is always a manager walking the 'racetrack,' making sure that customers are being served and shelves are being re-stocked when they should be. The managers deploy people from other departments, if necessary; and if a store manager isn't available, a zone manager or operation manager steps in. So the energy level never slips very far before someone gives it a boost.

"We're keeping up the maintenance of our stores. We have a zone recovery program that gets the store back to grand opening readiness every day. When you go into a store that is really cranking, doing maybe $900,000 a week, and even on Monday morning it's clean and the shelves are stocked—well, that's a joy to see. After all, we're in business to be busy!"

The Nineties have been very busy for Lowe's.

"**T**he decade began with a straightforward statement of Lowe's strategic mission," says Leonard Herring. Published in February of 1990, the mission statement was:

> **Lowe's is in the business of providing the products to help our customers build and improve their homes. Our goal is to be their 1st Choice Store for these products.**

1976
Emory Worley remembers that Lowe's used to give away monkeys and billy goats at grand openings. "Two thousand people would register to win a billy goat, although you could buy one for $3. Nobody really wanted it, but the publicity made it a big thing. The monkeys were always a success, because they would entertain everyone who came in the store."

Plant display at Lowe's of Baton Rouge.

It could have been written by Carl Buchan himself—and Carl Buchan would have loved the application of technology and manpower that has put more muscle in Lowe's mission every year.

Technology: it's the steam engine of our century, the tool that has changed the job for millions in the postwar era.

When we say technology today, we generally mean electronics technology, and we're generally thinking of computers. In 1946, the year that Carl Buchan and Jim Lowe started their collaboration in Lowe's North Wilkesboro Hardware, the first general-purpose electronic computer was built at the University of Pennsylvania. Fifty years later, Lowe's 56,000 employees are assisted by computers in almost every task that is performed between the front door and the rear loading dock, as well as at the general office.

Technology has also revolutionized Lowe's logistics department, which "is all about keeping our stores stocked," says senior vice president Lee Herring. "That's still the single most important service we offer our customers: they come to us for the products on our shelves.

"We can have the prettiest stores, the best salespeople, and the lowest prices; but if the product that a customer wants is not there, nothing else matters."

Lowe's distribution centers today bear little resemblance to the COW of yesteryear. The prototype for Lowe's latest generation of high-tech d.c.'s opened two years ago in North Vernon, Indiana. It features integrated systems for receiving, sorting, conveying, replenishing, order picking, and shipping. Its "carousel pick-and-pack" sounds like a carnival ride, but is actually a computer-driven system that allows Lowe's to ship precise quantities of a product instead of whole cases, so that stores receive exactly the

Areas of a 115,000-square-foot Lowe's store.

merchandise they need.

"Everything about it was new to Lowe's—the automation, the software systems, the building itself," says Lee. "In North Vernon, Lowe's made the leap from 1970's distribution technology to a state-of-the-art Nineties facility.

"In March of 1996, we opened a similar facility in east Texas. Our newest regional distribution center is in Statesville, North Carolina. Another is under construction in southern Georgia, and we're looking at sites for a fifth d.c. that we hope to open in 1998."

In the 1980's, there were three paths to retail success. You could get there by having the best prices, or by having the best selection, or by having the best service. Wal-Mart was the exemplar of success through everyday low pricing; Toys 'R' Us became known as *the* place to go for any toy, from Barbie dolls to Teenage Mutant Ninja Turtles; and for service *de luxe*, there was Nordstrom's or (depending on your ZIP code) Neiman Marcus.

No sooner had Lowe's begun to build big

Top: Lowe's Baton Rouge store on a Saturday morning.
Middle: Evangeline Spurlock of Lowe's Baton Rouge store.
Bottom: Tree Gilbert wields a scanner at Lowe's North Vernon distribution center.

stores than they realized that big boxes alone were no guarantee of success. Builder's Square had exploded onto the home center scene in the early Eighties, doing a billion dollars in sales within just a few years, but never making a meaningful profit. ("Anybody can make a big splash by throwing money out the window," says Leonard Herring.) Hechinger and HQ, who had big stores before Lowe's, have not been as successful in the long run. What Lowe's wanted was a recipe for success in the Nineties and beyond.

"It started with a challenge from Bob Tillman, who was senior vice president for merchandising in 1989," says Greg Wessling. The two Gregs, Wessling and Bridgeford, are now Lowe's chief merchants.

"Bob wanted us to get more products into the stores. Before long, we found that we were adding products faster than we could grow the square footage. The merchandise wouldn't fit on the sales floors. That led to larger stores: the sku count drove the sales floor size.

"We put teams together and went on the road. We went all over the United States and to Canada and Europe. We looked at other home centers to see what they were selling—what was attracting the customer's attention. That's what got us in the lawn and garden business. That's what got us seriously into home decor.

"We went pretty quickly from an average sales floor of 20,000 square feet in 1989 to today's big stores in the 115,000

1960

Max Freeman on Carl Buchan and the NFL: "I had flown Carl Buchan down to Miami, and we were both staying in a hotel. He called my room and said 'Why don't you come up here and meet these fellows?' And he gave me a suite number. So I went up there and found a group of men smoking cigars, and Carl said 'I've joined this group of people; we're going to bring professional football to Dade County.' And one of the fellows in the room was Joe Robbie. There were about six men, and Carl Buchan was in it with them. But he died before anything came of it."

Helping a customer get just the right color in the paint department.

class. And we weren't just loading them up with anything we could think of. We stopped carrying motorcycles and mopeds, camping gear, sporting goods, tents, pool tables, and boat motors. We had been doing a multi-million dollar business in bicycles, and we dropped that. It didn't fit Lowe's mission.

"The mission was what drove us when we started our quest for 40,000 sku's. We wanted to put together a store that would do $25 million a year."

It took Lowe's 36 years, from 1946 to 1982, to achieve its first billion-dollar sales year. In 1995, Lowe's home decor and lighting department alone did $1.5 billion in sales.

The right people are getting the right assortment into the right stores for Lowe's.

When Leonard Herring became president and CEO in 1978, Lowe's was essentially a small company doing big business. Leonard's main challenge was to develop Lowe's organizational structure so that it would not only keep pace but actually encourage further growth. The most difficult part of meeting that challenge was working out the human equation. Inevitably, some of the people who had contributed substantially to Lowe's earlier progress ran short of expertise to take the company forward. That tough reality has had to be faced more than once in the dynamic years since 1978.

Wendell Emerine had come to Lowe's with the acquisition of a store in Circleville, Ohio. Dwight Pardue became his mentor. In 1985, when Dwight left store operations to take charge of Lowe's real estate department, it was Wendell's turn at bat.

David Shelton worked with Wendell after moving to store operations from the training department. "Wendell was extremely well-read and knowledgeable," David recalls, "not only about Lowe's and the

Top: Effective advertising is a key to Lowe's success.
Bottom: A powerful department.

home center industry, but about retailing in general and the entire service sector of the economy.

"He encouraged us to be innovative in our merchandising. As a manager, he favored the team approach. He improved bonus programs by making sure they included everyone, not just the individual superstars who won awards."

In the second half of the Eighties, Wendell Emerine was the man for the job. By 1992, however, Lowe's had changed considerably. Sales had grown from $2 billion in 1985 to $3.8 billion. The total sales floor square footage had more than doubled, from 3.6 million to almost ten million. The number of employees had grown by more than fifty percent, from 13,000 to more than 21,000.

Leonard decided that Lowe's store operations needed someone with experience running a chain of large stores. This time, he looked outside Lowe's for a heavy hitter among other teams in the major leagues of retailing. He found Michael Rouleau, a midwesterner who had worked with Target, Dayton Hudson, and Office Warehouse. Rouleau came to Lowe's in the fall of 1992 as executive vice president for store operations.

"Michael Rouleau injected discipline and brought more

Top: Custom kitchen planning requires expert service.
Left: The wood cutting service is tremendously helpful to retail customers.
Below: You'd have to be blind to miss the window treatment area.

Lowe's NASCAR

Beginning in 1997, Lowe's will sponsor the car driven by Mike Skinner and owned by Richard Childress Racing. In 1995 and 1996, Lowe's and five of its best vendor companies (MTD Yard Machines, Owens Corning, Sylvania Lighting, Southeast Wood Treating, and Valspar Paints) have sponsored Brett Bodine's #11 Ford Thunderbird.

Says Lowe's Dale Pond, "NASCAR fans are among Lowe's most loyal customers. Surveys tell us that they visit Lowe's more frequently, and spend more with us than average.

"In Lowe's NASCAR partnership, everybody wins: Lowe's, its vendors, NASCAR, and the fans. It's a win-win-win-win situation."

centralized control to store operations," David Shelton says. "He refined operating details to a much greater degree than Wendell. He had a big impact on this company."

Rick Fitzgerald managed Lowe's Winston West store in Winston-Salem during the Rouleau years. "I learned a lot from Michael Rouleau about being in charge, being a leader," he says. "I learned how to create an atmosphere of excitement and enthusiasm in a store.

"How do you create a feeling that communicates to customers? That was something Rouleau emphasized. And we certainly missed the mark a lot in the beginning. There were times when [district manager] Robert Gragg and I were in the store with Michael Rouleau, and Rouleau would say 'I want to see you both in the training room.' That meant big-time trouble, and it happened more than once. Robert and I used to call them SCUD attacks, and we took some direct hits. But Rouleau knew what he was doing."

In 1992, Leonard Herring was also seeking a new computer and telecommunications wizard for Lowe's MIS (Manage-

> ### c.1950
> *Leonard Herring on accountability: "I remember an incident that occurred before I joined Lowe's, while I was working at Weil's in Goldsboro. The manager of the farm supply store ordered some water pitchers. On the order form he had written the number twelve, thinking he was ordering a dozen. Instead, he was ordering twelve dozen! For months, every time I saw him around town, he had a water pitcher under his arm. He sold those water pitchers one at a time until they were gone."*

ment Information Systems). He found Bill Irons, an econ grad out of the University of Tulsa who had been a management consulting partner with Ernst and Young.

Paula Anderson met her fiancé, Mark Kennedy, when they both worked at Lowe's. Thirteen members of Paula's family have been Lowe's employees.

Coach Herring had another big recruiting year in 1993, when he signed Greg Dodge to handle the increasingly widespread and complex functions of Lowe's real estate department. He also signed Bill Warden, a lawyer who had come to know Lowe's very well while working in the firm of Lowe's old friend Bill McElwee, who was now retired. Warden joined Lowe's as in-house general counsel and corporate secretary.

Another hot recruit was Dale Pond, a marketing phenom from Payless Cashways and Montgomery Ward by way of the Caribbean and HQ. Bob Strickland had met Dale when he was working for David Stanley at Payless, and Bob recommended him to Leonard. Dale joined Lowe's as senior vice president for marketing.

Marketing techniques in the Nineties reflect the application of technology that simply wasn't available just a few years ago.

"Until the Eighties, we didn't have the data we needed," Dale Pond explains. "There were no bar codes or other means of data collection, and we didn't have the ability to analyze data if we'd had it.

"More recently, we ran into another problem: there was no way to apply what we knew."

For instance, it is now possible to know that homeowners in a certain ZIP code have big lawns and tend to spend a lot on plants and gardening tools. Theoretically, Lowe's could target that ZIP code

Top: Lowe's 50th anniversary store managers' meeting in Nashville, 1996.
Bottom: Uncork the champagne! Lowe's grand opening in Champaign, Illinois.

20/20 Foresight

The year 2020 is closer to us now than 1970. Although this is a history, it would not be true to the impelling spirit of Lowe's past if it failed to look ahead—to theorize, to speculate, to entertain possibilities.

Many of the people who will lead Lowe's in 2020 already number among Lowe's 56,000 employees today. Here is a representative group who agreed to risk the laughter of posterity by taking a shot at describing what Lowe's will be like, twenty years into the new millennium:

From left to right:

Don Stallings- regional vice president of stores, Irving, TX
Karen Worley- vice president, managerial accounting
David Oliver- director, community relations
Dan Clemmens- store manager, Fayetteville, NC
Mike Menser- vice president, logistics
Mark Kauffman- director of import merchandise
Perry Jennings- vice president, human resources

Seated in front:

Eric Echols- regional loss prevention investigator
Tia Irving- district manager, Mt. Pleasant, SC
Sandy Dickerson- store manager, Ft. Walton Beach, FL
Robert Niblock- director of tax and regulatory reporting

with a newspaper insert dedicated to lawn mowers, trimmers, and garden center offerings. But the local newspaper has to be willing to distribute by ZIP code.

"We can be very discrete in our marketing and merchandising initiatives today," says Dale. "In fact, we could market to individual customers: we have the potential to know their specific interests.

"When marketing gets this discrete, it's very efficient—meaning we can lower costs and leverage our investment. In the Nineties, there has to be immediate, measurable payback for dollars spent on advertising.

"For years, Lowe's industry has been big, basic, growing, and fragmented. It's still big and basic—we still provide shelter, a basic need—but the growth curve is flattening.

"In the Seventies, the Baby Boomers were forming

Mark Kauffman: Today, Lowe's stocks a limited number of products—around 40,000—out of several hundred thousand out there. In the year 2020, Lowe's on the Internet could offer every item being manufactured, and throw in home delivery service direct from the manufacturer. **Perry Jennings:** Will we need big stores? If our job is to get it from the manufacturer to the consumer at the lowest price, do we even need to put it in a store? **Mike Menser:** What will be in large stores are the stock items that we carry today, with another 50,000 items available in one or two days on S.O.S. (Special Order System) from our distribution cen-

households at a tremendous rate. Now the pig is moving farther down the python, and new household formations are declining. Lowe's competition has gotten tougher. Weaker entries have fallen by the wayside. It's a two-horse race, and the battle is for market share. The competitors have to differentiate themselves.

"It's not enough to say 'Well, we're blue and they're orange.' When prices and products are as similar as they are now, the only differentiating element left is service—which services are offered, and the level of those services.

"Our 'Lowe's Knows' campaign addresses the issue of service, telling people that we have quality products priced right,

available from friendly, helpful, knowledgeable, reliable people.

"But it has to be more than an ad campaign. We have to deliver the goods in our stores."

Rick Fitzgerald on what really counts:

"It's not the objective things like sales figures and profits and the other numbers we all like so much; it's the subjective part of our business, the emotional part.

"You can treat employees like commodities. You can push them around, load them down with work, cut the payroll to the bone, go for productivity, productivity, productivity. I know; I've worked at places where that happens.

ters. People won't wait two weeks for delivery anymore. **Dan Clemmens:** Store size will cap out in the range of 150,000 to 175,000 square feet. Look at what Wal-Mart's done with the Hypermarts: they're not expanding that area. When I look at our customer base today, I see a real opportunity to serve the Repair & Remodeling guys, the small tract builders. **Tia Irving:** My vision is that we will continue with stores that are 135,000 to 150,000 square feet, stocked with basic home improvement requirements—but those will be different. Electrical and plumbing systems in houses of the future will be nothing like they are now. They'll be very sophisticated but very simple. Everything else—decor items, lighting fixtures, things that are not structural will be ordered through electronic networks either from home or from the store. No matter where the order originates, it will be shipped direct from the vendor to the customer. **Mark Kauffman:** There will be products on our shelves that aren't even made today. There will be environmentally friendly products that aren't available now. Pack-

"Lowe's isn't like that. Lowe's leadership understands that employees have to be treated with consideration and professional respect. It's through our employees that good customer service and superior customer satisfaction are generated.

"Our people drive this business for us."

Nick Canter on teamwork under fire:

"There was a disaster in my region on April 16, 1996,

A Garden of Eden- but with better shopping carts.

when our store in Albany, Georgia burned to the ground.

"Someone pulled me out of a meeting in North Wilkesboro and told me that I had a store emergency. My district manager, Mike Stokes, was calling from his car phone in the Albany parking lot, literally watching the store burn.

"His fear and concern ran like lightning through the

aging will be more environmentally friendly—in many cases, you'll see less packaging, or none at all. **Mike Menser:** There will certainly be less packaging. We don't have enough landfills. Products that weigh less also have lower shipping costs. **Mark Kauffman:** Also, the products used to build a home will

change. As less lumber is available and it becomes more expensive, more materials will be metal or plastic. But as we shift, the consumer will need to be educated. It happened in the shift from plywood to structural lumber. Lowe's will provide information to help sell the vendor's product. I think there'll be as much

general office. We commandeered jets from the company fleet, and within two hours I was on the scene.

"It was phenomenal how we rallied as a team to go to the aid of that store. People put aside everything else on their agendas. It was heartwarming to see: the pilots, the secretaries, the logistics folks, the merchandising staff, the loss-prevention people, the human resource people, the real estate people—it was amazing.

"Nobody was injured; that was the most important

1964
Lowe's had recently expanded its international sourcing. Unfortunately, some of the imported products were a little short on quality. Hal Church was standing by a bin of imported hammers one day when a woman customer stopped to exclaim, "Oh, look! Hammers for just 99 cents! How many do you think I should get?" Replied Church, "Well, ma'am, how many nails do you want to hit?"

Lowe's donates trees for planting projects.

thing. And the store's employees didn't lose any wages: we moved them around to other locations to insure their continued income.

"We got on the phone immediately to make plans with vendors. Lowe's real estate staff found a building that we could lease temporarily, and the very next day we had construction and engineering people checking it out. The next day, someone was in there to clean the floors. The next day, racks were set up. The next day, merchandise was delivered. We were back in business within eight days, and I don't think there was a harsh word spoken in any department at any level during the whole experience.

"The epitome of teamwork is when everyone pulls together through a crisis."

information as product in stores. **Tia Irving:** Stores will be plain and simple—no frills. The accessibility of large, bulky items will be more important than a high fashion presentation. **Karen Worley:** We'll have to carry products for which service makes a difference. Otherwise, why have us at all? If you can get on the Internet and order light bulbs and paint delivered to your house, then the

niche of the retailer will be the service side. **Tia Irving:** There will always be a need for service—to be the middle man, make sure an order is right, get things repaired. Someone has to be accessible to the customer, representing the vendor. **Perry Jennings:** Service—that's what we have to sell.

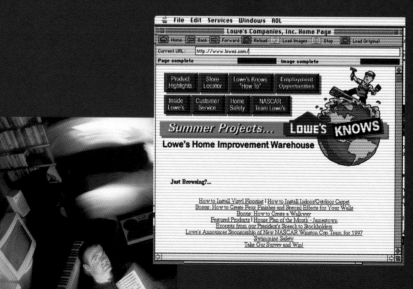

Lowe's Web Site
Launched in 1995, Lowe's home page at www.lowes.com is one of the most interesting and informative sites on the Worldwide Web. In 1996, it won the "Best Educational Value" category of the Best of the Web competition sponsored by Coopers & Lybrand.

Larry Stone on freedom with support:

"When I was a store manager, I always enjoyed the fact that I had this big company behind me, yet it was my store. As long as I made money, corporate would leave me alone.

"Of course, it was totally different when I was running the North Wilkesboro store. Everybody at the general office is the manager of that store!"

Our focus has to be on people, not tasks. **Sandy Dickerson:** We're going to need more partnership with our vendors in changing planograms, getting merchandise into the stores—stuff that our sales force is doing now. Someone has to be available to take care of the customer who has a problem.

Perry Jennings: There is also a huge opportunity in "contingent labor" who will come into a store for a week, do whatever it takes, then go on to the next store that needs them. But we have to get better at labor scheduling. **Dan Clemmens:** It's hard getting the quality individuals that we need to help customers on the sales floor.

The employment base is shrinking. It will help to have computerized kiosks throughout the stores, so that if someone needs a particular item, the kiosk can direct them. **Mark Kauffman:** There will be bar codes on every item, and when customers walk through the checkout, a machine will read every-

thing in their basket, and they'll be out the door. **Eric Echols:** Of course, the more technology we have, the more opportunities we create for fraud. With technol-

In 1969, Leonard Herring hired Larry Stone to work in the mail room at the general office for $1.60 an hour. In 1995, Larry became executive vice president for store operations, succeeding Michael Rouleau. Larry works most closely with Bob Tillman, who became chief operating officer in 1994.

Cliff Oxford had been running Lowe's investor relations department since 1984, building a reputation for unflappable authority among Lowe's institutional investors and analysts. Early in 1996, he became Lowe's senior vice president for corporate and human development.

For more than a decade, part of Cliff's job was to

Dr. Louis Sullivan (left), Bob Strickland, and Cliff Oxford at a meeting of the board of directors of Lowe's Home Safety Council.

ogy we get different types of crime. **Karen Worley:** When we have computerized checkout, we won't need cashiers. If we also have kiosks to do item search, we can run a store with a lot fewer employees. **Don Stallings:** You'll have more employees who are actually able to serve the customer. When they're not needed for tasks, they

can help in project areas, commercial sales, installation—areas that are labor-intensive. **Sandy Dickerson:** To help customers who use the Internet, I've got to have employees who know how to use the Internet them-

selves. That should be at least fifty percent of the employees in the store. **Perry Jennings:** We'll have much more diversity in our workforce. More multiculturalism. It's not go-

interpret Lowe's to the financial world. He is a painter of the big picture for Lowe's, and he sums up Lowe's current decade with an ease born of long practice.

"Since the early Nineties, we've had a three-tiered objective: price, selection, and service.

"The first thing we had to do was get our prices right. For years, so much of our total sales came from low-margin commodity products that we had to have higher prices on retail items in order to make any money at all. Competitors who had a lower percentage of commodities in their sales mix could have lower prices than Lowe's in the very categories where we wanted to compete.

"Bob Tillman became champion of the Everyday Low Price program, which was launched in 1991. Very quietly, category by category, we lowered prices on the products where we made our profit.

"It was whiteknuckle time. We were making these drastic price reductions,

1970

Mary Marsh on revelation: "During a Hootenanny in Atlanta, a hotel room caught fire in the night and all the guests, including Lowe's people, were called to the lobby. Nobody was injured and the damage was slight, but it was a sight to see all those employees frantically running around in their underwear!"

Greg Dodge (center), Lowe's senior vice president for real estate, met with community leaders in Statesville, NC in the planning stage of Lowe's new distribution center.

ing to be about physical task work; it's going to be about dealing with people. And store managers will be taking care of the people who are taking care of the customers. **David Oliver:** Technology will add incentives for customer service by making the salesperson identifiable on the sales receipt. The trend is toward better salesmanship. When we talk about fewer tasks and more customer service, it all gets very personal and interactive. **Don Stallings:** We need to give people what they're really after, more quickly. That's really important, in small towns as well as big cities. It will help us differentiate ourselves from others in the industry. **Mike Menser:**

Our stores in California won't look the same as our stores in North Carolina. Every store will carry different stuff—the right mix for that market. **David Oliver:** We can see differences now in Lowe's urban markets. We recognize that our store managers know the pecu-

and if sales didn't go up as a result, we were sunk. But our customers were smart: they noticed the change, and they responded.

"We put Everyday Low Prices in the hardware department, and stood back and waited. BOOM! Sales went up thirty percent and stayed up. Then we did the paint department; BOOM! Up a third! Electrical department; BOOM! In one category after another, when we lowered our prices, sales more than made up for it.

"The second tier was selection," Cliff continues. "Tillman, the two Gregs, and all the merchandising staff deserve a lot of credit for ramping up the sku count [getting a lot of merchandise!] in our big stores. Now our selection includes more high-end goods: better light fixtures, an incredible selection of wallpaper. The next wave will be special order goods. In the next millennium, we'll have 40,000 products on hand and possibly another 60,000 on screen that we can get for you by special order.

"The last tier—and frontier—is customer service. By the year 2000, Lowe's will have 100,000 employees. We want them to be the most highly skilled, best compensated, most enthusiastic sales force in the marketplace.

Tallahassee, Florida- An American Red Cross instructor teaches Lowe's employees how to help victims of respiratory failure.

liarities of their communities. They will help us know what needs should be addressed—both in terms of product mix and in terms of Lowe's corporate citizenship. As we continue to go into markets that don't know Lowe's at all, we'll find consumers demanding to do business with a company that gives back to the community. **Don Stallings:** We're expanding westward right now. Nationally speaking, California presents better opportunities than any we've encountered before. By 2020 we'll be looking international, at countries where we have most favorable trade agreements. We'll have new logistical and technical information at our finger-

tips. Right now, we worry about a van load having 80,0(pounds. By 2020, we'll be loading up container ship **Mike Menser:** I'm going to look at some ships this a ternoon. No, but really—Logistics today is about usir technology to cut waste and find better, cheaper way of getting the product where it needs to go. Lots of r

"Service only begins with things like cutting glass and pipe, helping customers load their cars. Service also means opening at 7:30 for our repair-and-remodel contractor customers. It means having the expertise to answer a customer's questions. It means being empowered to put aside a task or a routine in order to give special assistance. Service is an attitude.

"Leonard Herring says 'If you're not serving the customer directly, you'd better be serving someone who is.' For example, our sales force couldn't do their job without the technology provided by Bill Irons and the MIS folks. One way or another, we're all in customer service."

Bob Strickland was pondering ways for Lowe's to show its gratitude to the hundreds of communities that support its stores. He wanted something big-spirited and genuinely philanthropic; something that could be implemented in

Carol Farmer was elected to Lowe's board of directors in 1994.

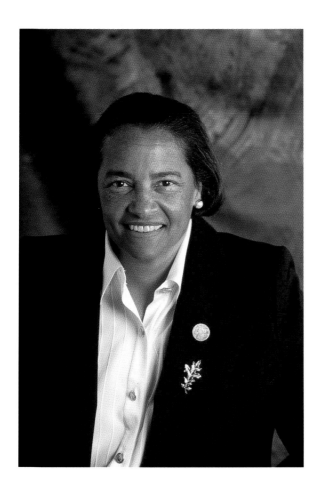

tailers are failing because they can't get product delivered at a reasonable cost, so what we're seeing is consolidation in the industry. And there's more coming. By 2020, there'll be fewer competitors, but the ones that exist will be stronger. Suppliers are going through the same thing. Suppliers will be conglomerates with lots of different product lines. **Karen Worley:** The future of management accounting is that by 2020 there will be less of it. Technology will make information instantly available to front line operators in the stores, and the same systems will enable management to measure productivity. It will be a two-way information supply. People like me will be working with the technology providers. **Robert Niblock:** Right now, the government is behind in the use of electronic document filing. We'll see more of that. Also, technology will expedite the interaction between stores and streamline the processing

all of Lowe's twenty-plus states; something that would touch all Lowe's customers, their families, and friends; something uniquely appropriate for Lowe's.

He had seen some statistics that caught his attention: each year, American homes are the scene of of nearly 20,000 accidental deaths and more than six million disabling injuries. These preventable incidents cost Americans roughly $85 billion a year.

Claudine Malone joined Lowe's "Boomer Board" in 1995.

Bob developed the idea for a Home Safety Council that would draw on the resources of Lowe's and its vendors and channel them into a variety of philanthropic projects. Each of Lowe's stores would become a home safety center, providing information and products to empower consumers to turn their homes into safe havens.

Lowe's Home Safety Council was established as a non-profit foundation in 1993. Its high-profile charter members included Lamar Alexander, Jack Kemp, and Dr. Louis Sullivan, as well as

Jack Shewmaker: "The new Lowe's suits the new decade."

of tax-exempt sales. **Don Stallings:** We have a store vehicle today that gives us a competitive advantage. We used to look for locations away from our competitors. Now the most appealing sites are right next to Home Depot or WalMart, because we have the right store, the right people, and the right prices. Lowe's future is in all the markets suited to our stores. **David Oliver:** You know, time and again, businesses are getting shut out of com-

munities. We talk about Lowe's being the retailer of choice for our customers, the employer of choice for our people, and the investment of choice for our stockholders. But we also need to be the neighbor of choice in Lowe's markets. That's why we started Lowe's Home Safety Council. By 2020, Lowe's stores will be *the* source for safety products and information, because we'll be in every community. We'll be the local outlet, and vendors will be helping us with our mission.

1977

Johnny Walker was going to give away a Pontiac Grand Prix to a store manager whose name would be chosen at random from among several who had met Walker's criteria. Bob Tillman and Greg Wessling both had their names in the hat. But although Walker got excited and gave away three cars instead of one, neither Bob nor Greg was a winner. Says Greg, "I was a little upset about it, so when I got home I went out and bought a car for myself. Bob was a little upset, and he went out and bought one, too! You didn't want to be the guy who didn't win the car."

national organizations such as the AARP and the National Safety Council.

In its first three years, the council sponsored television specials, gave home safety makeovers that drew media attention to the cause, set up a toll-free phone number with recorded safety information, installed interactive SafetyWatch kiosks in all Lowe's stores, and worked with local fire and police departments on community projects.

David Oliver, director of community relations, says "We just finished a retrospective video, and it made us think 'Wow, we really did all this!'

1996
Frank Beam on a good thing: "Give me someone for three years, and they'll be a Lowe's person forever."

The Champs: Bob Strickland and Leonard Herring with heavyweight George Foreman at Lowe's 1995 managers' meeting in Nashville.

"Lowe's Home Safety Council is our gift to Lowe's communities."

In 1992, the United States elected its first Baby Boomer president. The Baby Boom generation, that postwar pig in the population python, has entered its phase of highest earning power and greatest influence. Attended by hoopla and hype (as when have they not been?), Boomers are moving into the executive suites of private enterprise and taking up the reins of government. In the Sixties and Seventies, they redefined young adulthood; now they are dictating the terms of their maturity. Our institutions already reflect the passing of the leadership torch.

Lowe's big stores have been called "Boom boxes" for their popularity among Baby Boom customers. Today, most of Lowe's store managers are Baby Boomers, as are most members of the general office staff.

Lowe's board of directors, however, lacked Baby Boom

Pete Kulynych, with an old Lowe's ledger under his arm, remembers the original Lowe's store on C Street in North Wilkesboro.

representation. The board had always been exceptionally active and progressive; nevertheless, when the Nineties began, it was entirely composed of white males with an average age of 66.

"I began thinking that our board ought to look more like our customers," says Bob Strickland, "and not be just one gender, one generation, or one race. We needed more breadth."

Carol Farmer is a prominent futurist and retail strategist who had done some consulting for Lowe's in the Eighties. When Lowe's was making its big retail push, she helped give it force and focus.

"We were starting to think about the warehouse format, and wondering if we were going to need carpet—that kind of thing," says Bob. "Carol told us 'That's nonsense. A warehouse isn't a style statement, it is organizational efficiency. You don't need carpet; you need clean floors and great merchandise.'"

In 1994, Carol Farmer was elected to Lowe's board of directors. Another rookie on the board that year was fellow Baby

> **c. 1980**
> *A woman wanted to buy a ceiling fan to match one she already had. Lowe's salesman showed her everything in stock, then he showed her some that could be special-ordered; but still she hesitated. She was on the point of giving up when the salesman said "I've got it! Buy two: then you know they'll match!" And that's what she did.*

See No Evil, Hear No Evil, Speak No Evil: Executive secretaries Geraldine Bumgarner, Mary Marsh, and Linda McNeil have been with Lowe's for more than a hundred years, collectively. So why is it that none of them has any stories to tell?

Boomer Bob Tillman.

For further diversity, board member Bill Andres recommended a woman who had impressed him on other corporate boards. Claudine Malone was a Wellesley grad who had taught retailing at Harvard Business School. In 1995, she was deputy chairman of the Federal Reserve Bank of Richmond, Virginia and president of her own consulting firm in McLean. She had just rotated off the board of Scott Paper when Bob Strickland and Leonard Herring contacted her and asked her to be part of the "youth movement" on Lowe's board of directors. She laughed, accepted, and was elected in 1995.

Jim Halpin is the newest member of Lowe's "Boomer Board." He is the president and CEO of CompUSA, the chain of computer products superstores that currently records the highest sales per square foot of any major retailer in the country.

Although Jack Shewmaker left Lowe's board in 1994, he retains his interest in the board and the company. "I've sat on a number of boards, both standard and non-profit," he says, "and the quality of Lowe's board is exceptional. Although the members are from diverse backgrounds, they ask questions and are willing to participate. That should be the norm, but it's not.

"A different kind of board would never have agreed to Lowe's rapid expansion, with the huge increase in assortment. It was a big change from what was already working to what will work for the future.

"Lowe's board is exceptional because Bob and Leonard have sought people who would participate that way. It's been a significant component of Lowe's success."

In June of 1996, Leonard Herring announced the appointment of Tom Whiddon as Lowe's chief financial officer. Tom had been CFO of Zale Corporation, the Dallas-based jewelry retailer. Before

Gordon Cadwgan, who helped take Lowe's public in 1961, has been a lifelong friend and trusted advisor to Lowe's. He retired from Lowe's board of directors in 1996 and was elected director emeritus. He appears here with his daughter, Carol Lavell, and her dressage horse, Gifted. Carol and Gifted helped the U.S. Equestrian Team win a bronze medal in team dressage at the 1992 Olympic Games in Barcelona.

1970
When Walt McColl tried to demonstrate an insulation blower at a Hootenanny, he hit the wrong button and blew insulation all over the audience!

that, he was a vice president of the Eckerd drug store chain. He had plenty of experience with large retailers; Leonard, who had been Lowe's first financial officer, felt confident that Lowe's financial future would be in good hands with Tom.

With this important appointment, Leonard felt that he could say, as Carl Buchan had once said, "I've got my team together." On August 1, Leonard passed the torch of Lowe's leadership to the man who had been hired by Hal Church as a nineteen-year-old office manager trainee at the Raleigh store in 1962.

Bob Tillman had worked in Lowe's office and on the sales floor, in the mountains and on the coast. He had sold lumber to builders and bicycles to boys. He had run small stores and big stores, in boom times and bad. In the general office, he was respected for his successes; in the trenches, he was liked as one of the guys.

Says Leonard, "Bob Tillman knows better than anyone else where Lowe's needs to be and how to get there."

Top: Senator Russell Long, Congressional champion of ESOP's, with a group of Lowe's employees in Chantilly, Virginia.
Bottom: One of Lowe's youngest shareholders is Pete Kulynych's great-grandson Lance, born April 6, 1996. Left to right: Roena Kulynych, Russell Long, Pete Kulynych, John Belk (peeking), Laura Berry (Lance's mom), and Brenda Cline (Laura's mom).

Leonard Herring:
A Presidential Snapshot

At Lowe's annual meeting in May of 1996, President and CEO Leonard G. Herring announced his plans to retire. He had been Lowe's president and chief executive officer since 1978.

When he became president, Lowe's operated 199 stores in nineteen states, with total retail selling space of 1.8 million square feet. In 1996, the company has 375 stores in 23 states, and its retail space has grown to 25 million square feet.

In 1978, Lowe's did $800 million in sales.

In 1996, Lowe's sales will surpass $8 billion.

In 1978, Lowe's made $24 million in profits.

Last year, Lowe's made $226 million.

In 1978, retail sales were 40% of Lowe's business.

Last year, retail sales were 85% of total sales.

In 1978, shareholder equity was $140 million.

In 1996, it will reach $2 billion.

"Progress is the art of maintaining change in order, and order in change," Leonard Herring told the audience at Lowe's 1996 annual meeting. "If there's one dominant characteristic responsible for Lowe's success, it's been our ability to manage change.

"Not even a visionary like Carl Buchan could have predicted all the events that have influenced Lowe's growth," he continued. "However, I do believe that Lowe's of 1996 is a company that Carl Buchan would recognize, and of which he would be proud."

By the start of the new millennium, one hundred thousand people will be working for the company that began as a family hardware store in North Wilkesboro in 1946. Lowe's expects to more than double its current annual sales by the year 2000.

The members of Carl Buchan's team expect to enjoy that.

Pete Kulynych, Leonard Herring, Bob Strickland, and Bob Tillman in July of 1996.

Appendices

Lowe's success is an ongoing testament to the power of a great idea well executed. We think that artist Mel Steele's meditation on Lowe's roots is another great idea well executed, and we thought you would like to see it.

Appendix 1: Stock Splits and Dividends Since 1961

Here's what has happened to 100 shares of Lowe's stock bought for $12.25 per share on the initial offering date in 1961 and held as a long-term investment. At $32 per share, 12,000 shares have a market value of $384,000, or 313 times the original investment.

Date		Action	Shares Received	Total Shares
Oct.	1961	Bought 100 shares	100	100
May	1966	100% Dividend (2 for 1)	100	200
Nov.	1969	Stock Split (2 for 1)	200	400
Dec.	1971	50% Dividend (3 for 2)	200	600
Aug.	1972	33 1/3% Dividend (4 for 3)	200	800
June	1976	50% Dividend (3 for 2)	400	1,200
Oct.	1981	50% Dividend (3 for 2)	600	1,800
Apr.	1983	66 2/3% Dividend (5 for 3)	1,200	3,000
June	1992	100% Dividend (2 for 1)	3,000	6,000
Mar.	1994	Stock Split (2 for 1)	6,000	12,000

Appendix 2: Top 100 Employees, Hiring Date

Leonard G. Herring, 12/7/55
Arnold N. Lakey, 10/18/56
Robert L. Strickland, 6/14/57
Basil W. Walker, 7/23/58
Linda E. McNeil, 4/6/60
Roy L. Phillips, 6/6/61
Harold E. Moore, 6/15/61
Franklin V. Beam, 8/1/61
Charles B. Ballard, 6/4/62
Shelby H. Reeves, 6/13/62
Paula M. Bentley, 11/9/62
Robert L. Tillman, 11/12/62
Lana S. Johnson, 3/28/63
Walter G. Crews, 5/13/63
Geraldine M. Bumgarner, 5/22/63
James G. Joines, 3/2/64
John F. McGee, 5/25/64
Roy H. Boling, 5/24/65
Theodore L. Gaylor, 5/31/65
Houston G. Russell, 3/14/66
Roy C. Butler, 4/18/66
Gary M. Sparks, 6/6/66
Carol S. Mitchell, 7/11/66
Carol A. Triplett, 8/29/66
Billy L. Watts, 9/6/66

John C. Batten, Jr., 11/7/66
Brenda D. Sellers, 3/29/67
Clyde R. Monday, 4/24/67
Rita C. Adams, 5/15/67
Joyce B. Joines, 5/18/67
Martha H. Myers, 6/12/67
Charles M. Gentle, 7/31/67
James P. Parsons, 9/11/67
Harold Dean, 9/16/67
Jimmie W. Priddy, 9/25/67
James L. Chatham, 2/19/68
Roby S. Earp, Jr., 3/25/68
David H. Sain, 3/29/68
Noah J. Metz, 4/1/68
Linda G. Holbrook, 4/15/68
Junior W. Starliper, 4/29/68
Willie L. Dock, 4/29/68
Lane H. McGlamery, 6/18/68
Michael J. Boswell, 7/8/68
Mary M. Marsh, 8/19/68
Isaac Floyd, 8/26/68
Margaret A. Prevette, 9/23/68
Doris F. Combs, 10/14/68
Sylvia H. Burgess, 10/21/68
Dale J. Church, 1/20/69

L.C. Haynes, 3/10/69
Edwin R. Tharpe, 3/11/69
Walter L. McColl, 4/14/69
William L. White, 5/19/69
Debbie B. Poole, 6/2/69
Larry D. Stone, 6/2/69
Edward D. Parker, 6/14/69
Pauline R. McLean, 7/21/69
Savannah E. Williams, 7/21/69
Alvin L. Washington, 7/25/69
Robert A. Gragg, 7/31/69
Barbara K. Higgins, 8/11/69
Sandra L. Redman, 8/26/69
Donald D. Cairnes, 9/1/69
Freddie H. Washington, 9/16/69
Jesse F. Triplett, 9/26/69
Stephen Absher, 11/24/69
Michael R. Cothren, 12/3/69
James V. Johnston, 12/15/69
James H. Benson, 1/28/70
Joe L. Coates, 4/13/70
William W. Johnson, 4/13/70
Vickie Bauguess, 4/27/70
Evelyn S. Laws, 5/4/70
Fred A. Roope, 5/11/70

Arvil R. Mitchell, 5/20/70
Michael L. Faw, 5/28/70
Christopher D. Shumate, 6/2/70
Michael B. Hodges, 6/15/70
John E. Sugg, III, 6/15/70
Leland Baker, Jr., 7/13/70
William D. Pelon, 7/21/70
George A. Hart, Jr., 7/27/70
Luther Hunter, 8/1/70
Linda M. Johnson, 8/19/70
Larry J. Howard, 9/7/70
Melba J. Phillips, 9/23/70
Patsy A. Frady, 10/19/70
Raymond A. Rawley, 10/26/70
Jeremiah L. Davis, 10/29/70
Dennis T. Riggins, 11/2/70
Betty J. Wyatt, 11/10/70
Judy D. Bumgardner, 11/16/70
David E. Shelton, 11/16/70
Jimmie A. Cline, 11/23/70
Gerald W. Bodiford, 1/11/71
Wilton S. Waters, 1/18/71
Donald R. Bumgarner, 1/25/71
Fonda T. Parsons, 2/9/71

Appendix 3: Current Store Locations on August 1, 1996

Lowe's of Wilkesboro, N.C.
Lowe's of Sparta
Lowe's of S.E. Columbus, Oh.
Lowe's of Shawnee, Okla.
Lowe's of Columbus, Ind.
Lowe's of Winston-Salem
Lowe's of Columbia, Mo.
Lowe's of Bellefontaine, Oh.
Raleigh N.C. Ctr Yd
Lowe's of Lafayette, Ind.
Lowe's of Richmond, Va.
Lowe's of Staunton, Va.
Lowe's of Madisonville, Ky.
Chesapeake, Va. Ctr Yd
Lowe's of Fremont, Oh.
Lowe's of Lebanon, Pa.
Lowe's of Kingsport, Tenn.
Lowe's of Charleston, S.C.
Lowe's of Dover, Del.
Lowe's of Texas City, Tex.
Wilmington, N.C. Ctr Yd
Lowe's of Boone
Lowe's of Hendersonville, N.C.
Lowe's of Newnan, Ga.
Lowe's of Wilson
Myrtle Beach, S.C. Ctr Yd
Lowe's of West Columbus, Oh.
Newport News, VA, Ctr Yd
Lowe's of Suffolk, Va.
Lowe's of Whiteville
Lowe's of Dayton-Trotwood, Oh.
Lowe's of Charleston, W. Va.
Lowe's of Steubenville, Oh.
Lowe's of Lumberton
Lowe's of Benton Harbor, Mich.
Lowe's of Seneca, S.C.
Lowe's of Frankfort, Ky.
Roanoke, Va. Ctr Yd
Jacksonville, N.C. Ctr Yd
Lowe's of W. Ft. Wayne, Ind.
Lowe's of Cumberland, Md.
Lowe's of Augusta, Ga.
Lowe's of Burlington, Ia.
Chattanooga, Tn. Ctr Yd
Lowe's of De Kalb, Ill.
Lowe's of Burlington
Lowe's of Midland, Tex.
Lowe's of Lexington, Ky.
Lowe's of Washington
Lowe's of Martinsville, Va.
Lowe's of Dothan, Ala.
Lowe's of Battle Creek, Mich.
Montgomery, Ala. Ctr Yd
Lowe's of Goshen, Ind.

Lowe's of Ponca City, Okla.
Lowe's of Muscle Shoals, Ala.
Lowe's of Wichita Falls, Tex.
Lowe's of Tallahassee, Fla.
Lowe's of Sandusky, Oh.
Lowe's of Johnson City, Tenn.
Lowe's of Gastonia
Lowe's of Champaign, Ill.
Savannah, Ga. Ctr Yd
Lowe's of Lufkin, Tex.
Columbia, S.C. Ctr Yd
Lowe's of Jackson, Tenn.
Lowe's of Macon, Ga.
Lowe's of Virginia Beach, Va.
Lowe's of Adrian, Mich.
Lowe's of Beaver Creek, Oh.
Lowe's of San Angelo, Tex.
Lowe's of Corinth, Miss.
Lowe's of Galesburg, Ill.
Lowe's of Kannapolis
Lowe's of Louisville, Ky.
Lowe's of Beaumont, Tex.
Lowe's of Orangeburg, S.C.
Lowe's of Baytown, Tex.
Lowe's of Katy, Tex.
Spartanburg, S.C. Ctr Yd
Lowe's of Harrisonburg, Va.
Lowe's of Frederick, Md.
Lowe's of Bryan, Tex.
Lowe's of Moline, Ill.
Lowe's of Davenport, Iowa
Lowe's of Meridian, Miss.
Lowe's of Rome, Ga.
Lowe's of St. Clairsville, Oh.
Lowe's of Valdosta, Ga.
Lowe's of Midlothian, Va.
Lowe's of Sanford
Lowe's of Goldsboro
Lowe's of Muncie, Ind.
Lowe's of Dubuque, Ia.
Lowe's of Kankakee, Ill.
Lowe's of Belle Vernon, Pa.
Lowe's of Aiken, S.C.
Lowe's of Carencro, La.
Lowe's of Muskogee, Okla.
Lowe's of E. Ft. Wayne, Ind.
Lowe's of Sherman, Tex.
Lowe's of Waco, Tex.
Lowe's of Forest City
Lowe's of Marion, Va.
Teays Valley, W. Va. Ctr Yd
Lowe's of Thomson, Ga.
Lowe's of Gaffney, S.C.
Lowe's of Dublin, Va.

Lowe's of Reidsville
Lowe's of Lake Jackson, Tex.
Lowe's of Abilene, Tex.
Lowe's of Zebulon
Lowe's of Lincolnton
Lowe's of Mooresville, N.C.
Lowe's of N. Chattanooga, Tenn.
Lowe's of NW Indianapolis, Ind.
Lowe's of Jackson, Mich.
Lowe's of Laurens, S.C.
Lowe's of Maryville, Tenn.
Lowe's of Gallatin, Tenn.
Cincinnati, Oh. Ctr Yd
Lowe's of Inverness, Fla.
Lowe's of Albermarle
Lowe's of Thomasville, Ga.
Lowe's of Oxford, Ala.
Lowe's of New Iberia, La.
Lowe's of Warner Robins, Ga.
Lowe's of Chapel Hill
Lowe's of Greenwood, S.C.
Lowe's of Butler, Pa.
Lowe's of Cleveland, Tenn.
Lowe's of Peoria, Ill.
Lowe's of Hamilton, Oh.
Lowe's of Lancaster, Oh.
Lowe's of Kinston
Lowe's of South Boston, Va.
Lowe's of Texarkana, Tex.
Lowe's of Johnstown, Pa.
Lowe's of Greenville, N.C.
Lowe's of Statesboro, Ga.
Lowe's of Lake City, Fla.
Lowe's of S.W. Columbus, Oh.
Lowe's of Brunswick, Ga.
Lowe's of Denton, Tex.
Lowe's of Breckenridge, Va.
Lowe's of La Grange, Ga.
Lowe's of S. Baton Rouge, La.
Lowe's of Uniontown, Pa.
Lowe's of Franklin, N.C.
Lowe's of Cartersville, Ga.
Lowe's of Rockford, Ill.
Lowe's of Marion, Ill.
Lowe's of El Dorado, Ark.
Lowe's of Michigan City, Ind.
Lowe's of Natchitoches, La.
Lowe's of Indiana, Pa.
Lowe's of Heath, Oh.
Lowe's of Muskegon, Mich.
Lowe's of Mishawaka, Ind.
Lowe's of Vestal, N.Y.
Lowe's of Dayton Mall, Oh.
Lowe's of Westminster, Md.

Lowe's of Enid, Okla.
Lowe's of Wilmington Pike, Oh.
Lowe's of Killeen, Tex.
Lowe's of Zanesville, Oh.
Lowe's of Marion, Ind.
Lowe's of Mobile, Ala.
Lowe's of Corbin, Ky.
Lowe's of Salisbury, N.C.
Lowe's of Terre Haute, Ind.
Lowe's of Ashland, Ky.
Lowe's of Christiana, Del.
Lowe's of Temple, Tex.
Lowe's of Canton, Oh.
Lowe's of Gaithersburg, Md.
Lowe's of Elyria, Oh.
Lowe's of Erie, Pa.
Lowe's of Chambersburg, Pa.
Lowe's of Decatur, Ala.
Lowe's of Anderson, Ind.
Lowe's of Defiance, Oh.
Lowe's of Conroe, Tex.
Lowe's of Hammond, La.
Lowe's of Russellville, Ark.
Lowe's of Conway, Ark.
Millwork Redistribution Center
Lowe's of Stillwater, Okla.
Lowe's of Scranton, Pa.
Lowe's of S. Tulsa, Okla.
Lowe's of Trumbull County, Oh.
Lowe's of Decatur, Ill.
Lowe's of Ft. Oglethorpe, Ga.
Lowe's of Ft. Pierce, Fla.
Lowe's of Lima, Oh.
Lowe's of South Knoxville, Tenn.
Chester, Va. Ctr Yd
Lowe's of Springfield, Ill.
Lowe's of Houma, La.
Orlando, Fla. Ctr Yd
Lowe's of Marion, Oh.
Lowe's of Findlay, Oh.
Lowe's of Wooster, Oh.
Lowe's of Ontario, Oh.
Lowe's of Martinsburg, W. Va.
Lowe's of Dalton, Ga.
Lowe's of S. Oklahoma City, Ok.
Lowe's of New Philadelphia, Oh.
Lowe's of Amarillo, Tex.
Lowe's of Lubbock, Tex.
Lowe's of E. Indianapolis, Ind.
Lowe's of State College, Pa.
Lowe's of Gautier, Miss.
Lowe's of W. Indianapolis, Ind.
Lowe's of Columbus, Miss.
Greensboro, N.C. Ctr Yd

Lowe's of Joplin, Mo.
Lowe's of Reading, Pa.
Lowe's of Richmond, Ind.
Lowe's of Enterprise, Ala.
Lowe's of Victoria, Tex.
Lowe's of Southport, N.C.
Lowe's of Greeneville, Tenn.
Lowe's of West Augusta, Ga.
Charlotte, N.C. Ctr Yd
Lowe's of NE Indianapolis, Ind.
Lowe's of Taylors, S.C.
Lowe's of Churchland, Va.
Lowe's of Carrollton, Ga.
Lowe's of Bluefield, Va.
Lowe's of Crown Point, N.C.
Fredericksburg, Va. Ctr Yd
Lowe's of Wilmington, Oh.
Lowe's of S. Charleston, W. Va.
Lowe's of Lake County, Fla.
Lowe's of Banner Elk, N.C.
Lowe's of Middletown, Oh.
Lowe's of N. Knoxville, Tenn.
Lowe's of West Knoxville, Tenn.
Lowe's of Columbia, Tenn.
Lowe's of West Mobile, Ala.
Lowe's of Lexington, N.C.
Morgantown, W. Va. Ctr Yd
Lowe's of Southern Pines, N.C.
Lowe's of Cullman, Ala.
Lowe's of Somerset, Ky.
Lowe's of Jasper, Ala.
Lowe's of Cape Girardeau, Mo.
Lowe's of Athens, Tenn.
Lowe's of East Lexington, Ky.
Lowe's of Morehead City, N.C.
Lowe's of Lenoir, N.C.
Lowe's of Garner, N.C.
Lowe's of North Columbus, Ga.
Lowe's of Glasgow, Ky.
Lowe's of Concord, N.C.
Lowe's of Smithfield, N.C.
Lowe's of Holland, Mich.
Lowe's of Chapmanville, W. Va.
Lowe's of Florence, Ala.
Lowe's of West Asheville, N.C.
Lowe's of Sussex County, Del.
Lowe's of Henderson, N.C.
Lowe's of Galax, Va.
Lowe's of St Mary's County, Md.
Lowe's of Crossville, Tenn.
Lowe's of Tullahoma, Tenn.
Lowe's of Rio-Hill, Va.
Lowe's of Cross Lanes, W. Va.
Frederick, Md. Ctr Yd

Appendix 3: Current Store Locations Continued

Nashville, Tenn. Ctr Yd
Lowe's of Victorian Square, Va.
Lowe's of Elizabeth City, N.C.
Lowe's of Sumter, S.C.
Lowe's of Athens, Ga.
Lowe's of Summersville, W. Va.
Lowe's of Bartlesville, Okla.
Lowe's of Oxford Commons, N.C.
Lowe's of Acadiana Square, La.
Durham, N.C. Ctr Yd
Lowe's of Smoketown Station
Lowe's of Montoursville, Pa.
Lowe's of Kokomo, Ind.
Lowe's of Summerville, S.C.
Woodbridge, Va. Ctr Yd
Lowe's of Princetown, W. Va.
Lowe's of Hagerstown, Md.
Lowe's of Claypool Hill, Va.
Lowe's of Rocky Mount, N.C.
Lowe's of Morgantown, N.C.
Lowe's of Lake Charles, La.
Lowe's of Pine Bluff, Ark.
Lowe's of Danville, Ky.
Lowe's of Clarksville, Tenn.
Lowe's of Morgantown, W. Va.
Lowe's of East Asheville, N.C.
Lowe's of Monroe, N.C.
Lowe's of Hot Springs, Ark.
Lowe's of Murfreesboro, Tenn.

Lowe's of West Columbia, S.C.
Lowe's of Mt. Pleasant, S.C.
Lowe's of Tupelo, Miss.
Lowe's of Pineville, N.C.
Lowe's of Hickory, N.C.
Lowe's of Hattiesburg, Miss.
Lowe's of Hanover Crossings, Pa.
Lowe's of West Richmond, Va.
Lowe's of Longview, Tex.
Lowe's of Anderson, S.C.
Lowe's of Florence, S.C.
Lowe's of Irmo, S.C.
Lowe's of Greenville, S.C.
Lowe's of North Greensboro, N.C.
Lowe's of Fayetteville, N.C.
Lowe's of Rockingham, N.C.
Lowe's of Hermitage, Tenn.
Lowe's of Leesville, La.
Lowe's of Wise County, Va.
Lowe's of Morristown, Tenn.
Lowe's of Gadsden, Ala.
Lowe's of Cookeville, Tenn.
Lowe's of Richmond, Ky.
Lowe's of North Manassas, Va.
Lowe's of Pepperell Corners, Al.
Lowe's of Paintsville, Ky.
Lowe's of Easton, Md.
Lowe's of Shelby, N.C.
Lowe's of Charles County, Md.

Lowe's of South Savannah, Ga.
Lowe's of SW Greensboro, N.C.
Lowe's of Mechanicsburg, Pa.
Lowe's of Albany, Ga.
Lowe's of Winchester, Va.
Lowe's of North Charlotte, N.C.
Lowe's of Spartanburg, S.C.
Lowe's of Myrtle Beach, S.C.
Lowe's of Huntsville, Ala.
Lowe's of New Bern, N.C.
Lowe's of Madison, Tenn.
Lowe's of Jonesboro, Ark.
Lowe's of York, Pa.
Lowe's of Rock Hill, S.C.
Lowe's of NE Tallahassee, Fla.
Lowe's of SW Gainesville, Fla.
Lowe's of Roanoke, Va.
Lowe's of Newport News, Va.
Lowe's of Jacksonville, N.C.
Lowe's of Springfield, Mo.
Lowe's of Tuscaloosa, Ala.
Lowe's of Salisbury, Md.
Lowe's of Chattanooga, Tenn.
Lowe's of Cary, N.C.
Lowe's of Danville, Va.
Lowe's of Shreveport, La.
Lowe's of Owensboro, Ky.
Lowe's of Nashville, Tenn.
Lowe's of Alexandria, La.

Lowe's of Fayetteville, Ark.
Lowe's of N.E. Columbia, S.C.
Lowe's of Gainesville, Ga.
Lowe's of Pikeville, Ky.
Lowe's of Winston West
Lowe's of Lynchburg, Va.
Lowe's of Pensacola, Fla.
Lowe's of Chesapeake, Va.
Lowe's of Ocala, Fla.
Lowe's of S. Montgomery, Ala.
Lowe's of S. Indianapolis, Ind.
Lowe's of Beckley, W. Va.
Lowe's of North Raleigh, N.C.
Lowe's of University Centre
Lowe's of Altoona, Pa.
Lowe's of Christiansburg, Va.
Lowe's of Panama City, Fla.
Lowe's of Asheboro, N.C.
Lowe's of Monroe, La.
Lowe's of Bowling Green, Ky.
Lowe's of Bowie, Md.
Lowe's of Springfield, Oh.
Lowe's of Barboursville, W. Va.
Lowe's of Burlington, Oh.
Lowe's of Bristol, Va.
Lowe's of Franklin Square, N.C.
Lowe's of Statesville, N.C.
Lowe's of North High Point, N.C.

Lowe's of Elizabethtown, Ky.
Lowe's of N. Baton Rouge, La.
Lowe's of Ft. Smith, Ark.
Lowe's of Tyler, Tex.
Lowe's of Winchester, Ky.
Lowe's of Paducah, Ky.
Lowe's of Gulfport, Miss.
Lowe's of Orange City, Fla.
Lowe's of Allegany, Md.
Lowe's of Easley, S.C.
Lowe's of Waynesville, N.C.
Lowe's of Hagerstown, Md.
Lowe's of Chillicothe, Oh.
Lowe's of Wood County, W. Va.
Lowe's of E. Louisville, Ky.
Lowe's of Clarksburg, W. Va.
Lowe's of Fredericksburg, Va.
Lowe's of Wheelersburg, Oh.
Lowe's of Mt. Airy, N.C.
Lowe's of Ft. Walton Beach, Fla.
Lowe's of North Winston, N.C.
Lowe's of Augusta, Ga.
Lowe's of Ft. Oglethorpe, Ga.
Lowe's of Garner, N.C.
Lowe's of Lexington, N.C.
Lowe's of Albany, Ga.

Appendix 4: President's Managers of the Year

District Manager of the Year
1986 Frank Beam, Area 610
1988 Frank Beam, Area 610
1989 Fred B. Coates, Jr., Area 603
1990 John A. Raley, Area 619
1991 Phillip G. Stevens, Area 830
1992 Janice E. Lambert, District 811
1993 Basil W. Walker, District 815
1994 Charles Bruce Ballard, District 823
1995 Jack L. Way, District 852

Managers of the Year
1978
Charles DeBord, Manassas, VA
Bruce Ballard, Raleigh, NC
Frank Beam, Shelby, NC
Charles Jennings, Knoxville, TN
Jackie Holbrook, Hattiesburg, MS
1979
Jim Graves, Woodbridge, VA
Tom Farmer, Charleston, SC
Ed Roberts, Monroe, NC
Duke Belcher, Huntington, WV
Ron Higgins, Alexandria, LA
1980
Doug Campbell, Vienna, VA
Bob Tillman, Wilmington, NC
Dennis Brannon, Spartanburg, SC

Frank Bockeasy, Pikeville, KY
Denny Langston, Lake Charles, LA
1981
Mark Koch, Frederick, MD
David Sain, Hickory, NC
Lee Futch, Savannah, GA
Al Bullis, Johnson City, TN
Tom Yates, West Monroe, LA
1982
Ebbert May, Newport News, VA
Ray Ferguson, Hendersonville, NC
Jim Roberts, Thomasville, GA
Don Davis, Nashville, TN
George Andrews, Lafayette, LA
1983
Nick Canter, Charles County, MD
Dennis Sprinkle, Durham, NC
Keith Benson, College Park, GA
Roger Dotson, Pikeville, KY
Pat Arcement, Alexandria, LA
1984
John Raley, Morgantown, WV
Larry Stone, North Wilkesboro, NC
Harold Raynor, Jr., Aiken, SC
Bill Marshall, Morristown, TN
Robert Baureis, Jonesboro, AR

1985
John Rhea, Fredericksburg, VA
Sheldon Campbell, Wilson, NC
Luby Wood, Gastonia, NC
1986
Hylbert Riley, Harrisonburg, VA
Darrell Franks, Hendersonville, NC
Alan Ball, Nashville, TN
1987
John Haughton, Hanover, PA
Bill Pelon, Wilmington, NC
Tom Akins, Ft. Oglethorpe, GA
1988
William B. Johnson, Hagerstown, MD
William S. Leek, Rock Hill, SC
Terry L. Waterbury, Tupelo, MS
1989
Phillip Allen McNeil, Danville, VA
Tony C. Eller, Albermarle, NC
George E. Jones, Cookeville, TN
1990
John T. Adams, Morgantown, WV
Rollie A. Huffstetler III, W. Columbia, SC
Charles H. Bordwine, Claypool Hill, VA
1991
Carl D. Turner, Frederick, MD
Ronald G. Bullard, Lumberton, NC
Eric K. Barnes, West Monroe, LA

Ralph R. Herring, Gainesville, GA
1992
Terry L. Britt, Jacksonville, NC
Darwin C. Davis, Acadiana Square, VA
James W. Merrill, Parkersburg, WV
Robert G. McAnally, Orangeburg, SC
1993
David E. "Mickey" Holley, Lynchburg, VA
F. Lee McConnell, University Centre, NC
James A. Chaffman III, Greenwood, SC
Ricky D. Damron, Johnson City, TN
Marty L. Aynes, Tyler, TX
Paul R. May, Woodbridge, VA
1994
David W. Ashman, Christiana, DE
Claude G. King, Fayetteville, NC
William E. Smith, Macon, GA
Ricky D. Damron, Johnson City, TN
Richard A. Gortler, Clarkesville, TN
James R. Miller, Wilmington, NC
1995
Michael J. Boswell, Roanoke, VA
Richard S. Fitzgerald, Winston-Salem, NC
Sandra A. Dickerson, Panama City, FL
Gary L. Scriever, Altoona, PA
Kent E. Phillips, Springfield, MO
Timothy W. Anderson, Durham, NC

Appendix 5: Lowe's Management on August 1, 1996

Robert L. Strickland, Chairman Of The Board
Leonard G. Herring, Past President And CEO
Robert L. Tillman, President And Chief Executive Officer
Larry D. Stone, EVP Store Operations
William C. Warden Jr., EVP, General Counsel, Secretary
    And Chief Administrative Officer
Lee Herring, SVP Logistics
William L. Irons, SVP Management Info Services
Dale C. Pond, SVP Marketing
John G. Dodge, SVP Real Estate/Eng & Const
W. Cliff Oxford, SVP Corporate & HR Development
Richard D. Elledge, SVP/CAO/Asst Secretary
Gregory M. Bridgeford
    SVP/ General Merchandise Manager
Gregory J. Wessling, SVP/General Merchandise Manager
William D. Pelon, Regional VP Of Stores
Douglas L. Bowen, Regional VP Of Stores
Nick Canter, Regional VP Of Stores
Don T. Stallings, Regional VP Of Stores
William L. White, Regional VP Of Stores
Frank Beam, Regional VP Of Stores
John W. Vining Jr., VP Administration
James C. Neustadt, VP Advertising
Charles B. Ballard, VP Contractor Yard Operations
Arnold N. Lakey, VP Credit
Perry G. Jennings, VP Human Resources
Robert D. Skees, VP Internal Audit
Michael K. Menser, VP Logistics
Robert G. Oberosler, VP Loss Prevention
Karen R. Worley, VP Managerial Accounting
R. Vaughn Hayes, VP Merchandising Admin
Edward C. Seemann, VP MIS Systems Development
David E. Shelton, VP Store Operations
Kenneth A. Neal, Assistant Treasurer
Terry S. Carroll, Construction Director
J.D. Pardue, Construction Director
Kenneth W. Black, Jr., Controller
David E. Tyler, Dir Advertising Production
Clyde R. Monday, Dir Corp Credit Administration
Mickey N. Boyles, Dir Corp Credit Approv & Coll
Freddie T. Graves, Dir Corp Credit Approv & Coll
Theodore L. Gaylor, Dir Corp Credit Approv & Coll
Michael G. Elmore, Dir Distributed System Ops
Geoffrey B. Pagett, Dir Employee Services
Stephen L. Cox, Dir Human Resources Planning
Gary E. Whitman, Dir Human Resources-Stores
Hardy D. Wooten, Jr., Dir MIS Administrative Service
Robert C. Hicks, Dir Of Logistics Planning
Joseph E. Griffin, Dir Of Proj Planning/Design
Jeffery L. Osborne, Dir Pricing Administration
James S. Caudill, Dir Procurement/Supply/Distrib
Robert J. Grimsley, Jr., Dir R/E Prop Mgt/Excess Prop
Raymond A. Rawley, Dir Retail Credit/Direct Mkt
Carlton N. Lawson, Dir Spec Centers & Reloads

Robert A. Niblock, Dir Tax And Reg Reporting
Steven W. Palmer, Dir Transportation & Dist Syst
Rachel H. Jordan, Director Accounting Support
William F. Arrowood, Director Business Systems
Carol E. Perdue, Director Business Systems
Dennis L. Watkins, Director Business Systems
Jay A. Essary, Director Business Systems
Craig D. Jarrett, Director Business Systems
David J. Oliver, Director Community Relations
Gary E. Wyatt, Director Corporate Research
Warren L. Shinker, Director Facility Operations
William M. Watts Jr., Director Financial Planning
Andy T. Collins, Director Fleet Management
Donald B. Mulnix, Jr., Director General Accounting
Steven M. Stone, Director IRM
Billy E. Shomaker, Director Of Aviation
Daphne M. O'Keefe, Director Of Financial Analysis
Timothy H. Hauser, Director of Store Audit
John G. Spencer, Director Print Communications
William E. Hoffman, Director Real Estate
David D. Shomaker, Director Real Estate
Stanley C. Hostetter, Director Real Estate
William T. Renton, Director Real Estate Research
Allan S. Nelson, Director Sales Administration
Robert B. Harrell, Director Sales Planning
Ted S. Hagaman, Director Sales Promotion
Mitchel L. Franklin, Director Site Assessment
Leonel Anguiano, Director Store Loss Prevention
Troy G. Harmon, Jr., Director Store Set-Up
Alton L. Absher, Jr., Director Technical Development
Mark P. Koch, Director Vendor Logistics
Larry N. Christenbury, Director Vendor Logistics
Wade E. Sanders, Director Vendor Logistics
James M. Frasso, District Manager
Clifford W. Carroll, District Manager
Dwight H. Cabaniss, District Manager
Robert A. Gragg, District Manager
James L. Parker, District Manager
Matthew B. Thompson, District Manager
Tony W. Creech, District Manager
David H. Sain, District Manager
Teddy J. Hudler, District Manager
Claude G. King, District Manager
Barry E. Cox, District Manager
William W. Edwards, District Manager
Steven M. Stokes, District Manager
Robert D. Baureis, District Manager
David E. Ott, District Manager
Donovan W. Blackburn, District Manager
Bruce A. Seton, District Manager
Ricky D. Damron, District Manager
Mike Bryant, District Manager
Bruce E. Hokanson, District Manager

Richard S. Fitzgerald, District Manager
Kent E. Phillips, District Manager
Douglas E. Hartley, District Manager
James A. Chaffman III, District Manager
Terry L. Britt, District Manager
John K. Williams, District Manager
Donald G. Raynor, District Manager
Theresa C. Irving, District Manager
Michael J. Boswell, District Manager
Phillip G. Stevens, District Manager
Basil W. Walker, District Manager
David W. Ashman, District Manager
Terrance C. Delaney, District Manager
Daniel J. Georgiana, District Manager
Darwin Davis, District Manager
Marty Aynes, District Manager
Steven L. Hays, District Manager
Robert G. McAnally, District Manager
William E. Hibbs, District Manager
William S. Leek, District Manager
Connie D. Skidmore, District Manager
Gary P. Snyder, District Manager
Ronnie E. Damron, District Manager
Tony L. Starliper, District Manager
Janice E. Lambert, District Manager
Fred B. Coates, Jr., District Manager
John L. Kasberger, Divisional Merchandise Mgr
Mark A. Kauffman, Director of Import Merchandise
John R. Knight, Divisional Merchandise Mgr
Ray D. Benfield, Divisional Merchandise Mgr
Mike Smith, Divisional Merchandise Mgr
Michael K. Brown, Divisional Merchandise Mgr
Robert M. Joines, Divisional Merchandise Mgr
Eric D. Sowder, Divisional Merchandise Mgr
John D. Steed, Divisional Merchandise Mgr
Douglas E. Godwin, Divisional Merchandise Mgr
Steve M. Eller, Divisional Merchandise Mgr
James E. Abbott, Jr., Divisional Merchandise Mgr
Jeffrey E. Gray, Senior Corporate Counsel
Gaither M. Keener, Jr., Senior Corporate Counsel
Kevin D. Bennett, Senior Corporate Counsel
Danny L. Pardue, Senior Director Real Estate
W. Nathan Mitchell, Sr Dir Accounting
Edwin R. Tharpe, Sr Dir Accounting
Lewis E. Wilson, Sr Dir Distribution Ops
William E. Sammon, Sr Dir Eng & Construction
Roby S. Earp, Jr., Sr Dir Store Set-Up/Equipment
Dwight P. Ford, Sr Dir Training & Development
Michael R. Lyon, Sr Director Data Center Svs
Edgar M. Spears, Jr., Sr Director HR Operation
Lyle W. Paradise, Sr Director Risk Management
Scott Plemmons, Sr Director Store Operations

Appendix 6: Buchan Club Members

B.J. Bare
Frank Beam
Robert E. Black, Jr.
Clyde R. Brown, Jr.
George A. Brown, Jr.
Michael D. Brown
Virgil Bumgarner
Ross J. Burgess, Jr.
Alex Busick
Rome Christie
Bill Cockerham
William D. Cothern
Jerry Craven
Don Davis
B.H. Davis

A. Lee Deal
Les Dyer
Glenn Early
Phillip Fagg
Timothy L. Faw
Harold Ferguson
Kenneth L. Ferguson
Max J. Freeman, Jr.
Otis E. Giffin
Boyce Glenn, Jr.
Freddie Graves
Gordon L. Greene
Vernon Greene
Edward F. Greene

Robert A. Gresham, Jr.
J.A. Grisette
Claude Harmon
Gerald Hendley
James E. Holder
Charles H. Jennings
Dean Joines
Arnold Lakey
Jim Mauney
Jan McGee
W. Kyle McNeil
Wiley McNeil
James Miller
Jerry A. Miller

Paige R. Murray
Mailon Nichols
Dwight E. Pardue
Billy L. Phillips
Melvin Proffit
Herman Province
Charles E. Pugh
Edith B. Richardson
Edward Rizoti, Jr.
James Smith
John C. Stowe
Amon Swanger
J. Fred Walters, Jr.
Luby E. Wood

Acknowledgements

~

*Henry Church, Deni McIntyre, and Will McIntyre
offer their thanks to the following people,
without whose good-humored assistance
this book would not be this book.*

Stephanie Bass
Mike Brown
John Buchan
Ralph Buchan, Jr.
Faye Byrd and her staff at the Wilkes Community College Library
Nancy Canter
Rome Christie
Brenda Cline and Roena Kulynych
Lyn Church
Max Freeman
Rose Marie Gladieux
Kathleen Hartley
Alice Long
Lucy Lowe
Jeff McGill and Sarah McGill
Mabel McIntyre
Marge and Dan Pearson
Gary Wood

&

Lowe's 56,000 Employees

~